Thrive Online
A Guide to Remote Work and Digital Entrepreneurship
By
Mike Smith

Thrive Online

Michael Smith

Published by Michael Smith, 2024.

THRIVE ONLINE

First edition. April 6, 2024.

Copyright © 2024 Michael Smith.

ISBN: 979-8224263288

Written by Michael Smith.

Table of Contents

UNLEASH YOUR POTENTIAL Working from Anywhere by Building a Fulfilling and Flexible Online Career

In today's fast-paced digital world, the internet has opened up a vast array of opportunities to earn money from the comfort of your own home. Whether you're looking to supplement your regular income, escape the daily grind of a 9-to-5 job, or build a full-time online business, the potential is virtually limitless.

However, navigating the online world can be overwhelming, with countless promises of "get-rich-quick" schemes and dubious money-making opportunities. It's easy to fall prey to scams or waste time and effort on strategies that simply don't work.

That's where this book comes in. Drawing from years of experience and research, I've curated a comprehensive guide to help you identify legitimate, sustainable ways to generate income online. From freelancing and affiliate marketing to e-commerce and blogging, we'll explore a wide range of proven strategies that have helped countless individuals achieve financial success.

But this book isn't just a collection of money-making ideas; it's a practical roadmap to help you turn those ideas into action. You'll find step-by-step instructions, valuable tips, and real-life case studies to illustrate what works (and what doesn't) in the world of online income generation.

Whether you're a complete beginner or an experienced entrepreneur, this book will equip you with the knowledge and tools you need to navigate the digital landscape and unlock your full earning potential. We'll cover everything from identifying your unique skills and strengths to building a loyal audience, managing your time effectively, and staying ahead of the curve in an ever-evolving online ecosystem.

Making money online is not a get-rich-quick scheme; it requires dedication, perseverance, and a willingness to learn and adapt. But with the right strategies and mindset, the rewards can be truly life-changing – financial freedom, flexibility, and the ability to pursue your passions while earning a sustainable income. The internet has revolutionized the way we work. Today, with a computer and an internet connection, you can ditch the traditional office job and carve your own path to financial freedom. This book will be your guide on this exciting journey, exploring the many lucrative opportunities available in the vast online landscape.

Whether you're a seasoned professional with marketable skills or a complete beginner eager to learn, there's a place for you in the online economy. This book will unveil a variety of proven methods for generating income online, catering to different interests and skillsets.

We'll delve into the world of freelancing, where you can leverage your existing skills to work on projects from the comfort of your home. For the entrepreneurial spirit, we'll explore the exciting world of e-commerce, where you can build your own online store or sell handcrafted goods.

Do you have a passion you love to share with the world? We'll show you how to turn that passion into profit through content creation, allowing you to build an audience and establish yourself as an authority in your niche.

But what if you're just starting out and unsure where your strengths lie? Fear not! We'll explore a range of options that require little to no upfront investment, allowing you to test the waters and discover hidden talents.

This book goes beyond simply listing methods for making money online. We'll equip you with the knowledge and strategies you need to thrive in the digital marketplace. You'll learn how to build a loyal audience, identify profitable niches, and implement effective monetization techniques.

So, put on your virtual hat, grab your favourite cup of coffee, and get ready to embark on an enriching journey towards financial independence. With the right guidance and unwavering determination, you can turn your online hustle into a sustainable and rewarding career.

Let's embark on this journey together. By the end of this book, you'll have a clear understanding of the opportunities available, the skills required, and a personalized action plan to start generating income online and achieving your financial goals.

Are you ready to take control of your financial future? Let's get started!

The Allure of Working Online

THE TRADITIONAL OFFICE environment is undergoing a dramatic transformation. Gone are the days of rigid schedules, long commutes, and limited work-life balance. The rise of the internet and advancements in technology have opened doors to a new era of work – the era of online work. This chapter delves into the many advantages of working online, exploring the flexibility, freedom, and opportunities it offers for individuals seeking a more fulfilling and dynamic work experience.

The Allure of Flexibility

Work from Anywhere: Untethered from a physical office, online work allows you to set up your workspace wherever you have a reliable internet connection. Imagine working from a co-working space in a bustling city, a cozy coffee shop, or even the comfort of your own home – the choice is yours!

Set Your Own Schedule: Say goodbye to the tyranny of the 9-to-5 workday. Online work often offers greater control over your schedule. Whether you're a morning person or a night owl, you can structure your workday around your peak productivity hours and personal commitments.

Improved Work-Life Balance: Eliminate the daily commute and free up valuable time for personal pursuits. Working remotely allows you to integrate work seamlessly with your life, fostering a healthier balance between professional goals and personal well-being.

Unleashing Freedom and Control

Be Your Own Boss: For many, the dream of being their own boss is a powerful motivator. Online work empowers you to take control of your career path. Whether you're freelancing, building your own online business, or working remotely for a company, you have the freedom to choose the projects you work on and how you structure your workday.

Global Opportunities: The online world transcends geographical boundaries. Working online opens doors to collaborating with clients and colleagues from across the globe, fostering a diverse and enriching work experience.

Location Independence: Imagine living a nomadic lifestyle, traveling the world while you work. Or perhaps you dream of a life by the beach or a quiet mountain town – online work allows you to choose where you live without being restricted by a physical workplace.

Beyond Flexibility
Additional Advantages of Working Online

Reduced Expenses: Eliminate commuting costs and professional attire expenses associated with traditional office environments. Working from home or a co-working space can lead to significant cost savings.

Increased Productivity: Studies have shown that remote workers can be more productive than their office counterparts. A distraction-free environment and the ability to work during peak productivity hours can significantly enhance focus and output.

Environmentally Friendly: By reducing commuting and reliance on physical office spaces, online work can contribute to a more sustainable work environment.

The Bottom Line:

Working online offers a compelling alternative to the traditional office environment. It empowers individuals to embrace flexibility, take control of their careers, and achieve a better work-life balance. Whether you're a seasoned professional or just starting out, the online world presents a plethora of opportunities to build a fulfilling and rewarding work life on your own terms. This chapter has merely scratched the surface of the advantages of working online. The following chapters will delve deeper into specific online work options, explore the skills needed to thrive in this digital landscape, and offer practical guidance on navigating the exciting world of remote work and online entrepreneurship.

Different Ways
to Make Money Online:

◇ **Freelancing:** This is a great option for those with existing skills to offer, like writing, graphic design, programming, or even virtual assistance. You can find freelance work on platforms like Upwork, Fiverr, or Freelancer.com.

◇ **Selling Products Online:** There are many ways to do this. Consider dropshipping, where you manage the storefront but a third party warehouses and ships the products. You can also sell handmade crafts on Etsy or used items on eBay or Facebook Marketplace.

◇ **Content Creation:** This can be through a blog, a YouTube channel, or even a podcast. By building an audience, you can earn money through advertising, affiliate marketing, or selling your own products or services.

◇ **Online Courses & E-books:** If you have expertise in a particular area, you can create and sell online courses or eBooks. There are platforms like Udemy or Skillshare for courses, and Amazon Kindle Direct Publishing for eBooks.

◇ **Other Options:** There are many other ways to make money online, including taking surveys, testing websites and apps, or even playing games. However, these tend to have a lower earning potential.

Considerations for Success:

◇ **Building an Audience:** Regardless of the method you choose, focus on building an audience for your work. This will be key to your success.

◇ **Finding Your Niche:** There's a lot of competition online. Focus on a specific niche where you can provide unique value.

◇ **Monetization Strategies:** Explore different ways to monetize your online work. This could be through advertising, affiliate marketing, selling products or services, or subscriptions.

◇ **Time and Effort:** Building a successful online income stream takes time and effort. Be realistic about your expectations and committed to putting in the work.

Additional Tips:

◇ **Focus on Legitimate Methods:** There are scams out there that promise quick and easy money online. Avoid these and focus on legitimate methods.

◇ **Taxes:** Be aware of the tax implications of earning money online. Consult with an accountant if necessary.

◇ **Security:** Be mindful of online security when conducting business online.

BE YOUR OWN BOSS IN the Online World. Freelancing offers the freedom and flexibility to work on projects you choose, set your own hours, and be your own boss. If you have marketable skills – writing, graphic design, programming, virtual assistance, or even social media management – freelancing can be a path to a fulfilling online career.

This section will equip you with a step-by-step approach to launching your freelance career, from identifying your niche to landing your first paying client.

Step 1: Find Your Niche and Define Your Services

The freelancing landscape is vast. To stand out, specialize in a specific niche where your skills and experience can provide targeted value to clients.

Actionable Tip:

◈ Make a list of your skills and past experiences.

◈ Research online marketplaces like Upwork or Fiverr to identify in-demand skills within those areas.

◈ Consider your interests and passions – can you combine them with your skills to create a unique niche?

Real-Life Case Study:

Sarah, a graphic designer with a love for travel, identified a niche in creating custom travel brochures and social media graphics for tourism companies. This combination of her design skills and travel knowledge allowed her to target a specific client base.

Step 2: Build a Portfolio that Showcases Your Skills

A strong portfolio is your calling card in the freelance world. It demonstrates your skills, experience, and design aesthetic to potential clients.

Actionable Tip:

◈ If you're new to freelancing, create a portfolio website showcasing your best work, even if it's from personal projects or volunteer work.

◈ Don't have a website? Utilize online portfolio platforms like Behance or Dribbble.

◈ Tailor your portfolio to your niche by including projects relevant to your target client

Building Your Freelancer Portfolio:
Showcasing Your Skills. When you're new to freelancing, the biggest hurdle can sometimes be proving your skills and experience to potential clients. This is where your portfolio comes in – it's your digital storefront, a platform to showcase your best work and convince clients you're the perfect fit for their needs.

Here are some actionable steps to build a strong portfolio that gets you noticed, even if you're just starting out:

o **Craft a Compelling Website (Optional):** if you have the resources, consider creating a dedicated website to showcase your portfolio. This gives you complete control over the design and presentation, allowing you to tailor it to your unique brand and niche.

o Include high-quality visuals of your work, clear descriptions of your projects, and testimonials from satisfied clients (if available).

o Don't worry if you're not a web developer – there are plenty of user-friendly website building platforms available that can help you create a professional-looking website with minimal technical knowledge. These platforms offer a drag-and-drop interface, pre-designed templates, and a wide range of features, making them ideal for anyone who wants to establish an online presence without needing to write a single line of code.

Here are some examples of popular user-friendly website building platforms, along with their strengths:

◈ **Squarespace:** Known for its beautiful, clean templates and intuitive interface, Squarespace is a favourite among creative people and small businesses. It offers powerful features for building stunning websites with galleries, online booking systems, and e-commerce functionality.

◈

◈ **Wix:** Wix boasts a massive library of templates across various industries and a user-friendly drag-and-drop editor with extensive customization options. It's a great choice for those who want complete creative control over their website's design. Wix also offers built-in marketing and SEO tools to help your website get discovered online.

◈

◈ **GoDaddy:** A popular domain registrar and web hosting provider, GoDaddy also offers a user-friendly website builder with a focus on speed and ease of use. It's a great option for beginners who want a quick and straightforward way to get a website up and running.

◇ **Hostinger:** This affordable website builder offers a good balance of features and ease of use. Hostinger provides a user-friendly interface with pre-designed templates and an AI-powered website creation tool that streamlines the process for beginners.

◇ **WordPress.com:** A hosted version of the popular WordPress blogging platform, WordPress.com offers a user-friendly interface and a wide selection of free and premium themes. While it has limitations compared to self-hosted WordPress, it's a great option for those who want to create a blog or simple website without managing hosting and technical aspects.

Remember, the best platform for you will depend on your specific needs and goals. Consider factors like the type of website you want to build, your budget, your tech skills, and the features that are most important to you. Many website builders offer free trials or plans with limited features, allowing you to experiment and find the platform that feels most comfortable before committing.

◇ **Leverage Online Portfolio Platforms:**

o If creating a website isn't feasible, there are excellent online portfolio platforms specifically designed for freelancers. Popular options include Behance and Dribbble. These platforms allow you to create a profile, upload your work samples, and connect with potential clients and other creatives.

o

o **Behance:** This platform is a favourite among graphic designers, web designers, and other creative professionals. It offers a sleek, visually-driven interface perfect for showcasing your design projects.

o

o **Dribbble:** This platform caters more towards web designers, UI/UX designers, and animators. It's a community-driven platform where designers can share their work and get feedback from others.

Tailor Your Portfolio to Your Niche:

THE KEY TO A SUCCESSFUL portfolio is showcasing work relevant to your target clients. Don't just throw everything you've ever done on there. Instead, curate a selection of projects that directly demonstrate the skills and experience you're offering as a freelancer.

For example, if you're a freelance writer specializing in travel content, don't include blog posts on finance or technology. Instead, focus on travel articles, blog posts, or website copy you've written.

Bonus Tip:

Showcase the Process: Consider including snippets or mock-ups that showcase your creative process. This can give potential clients a glimpse into how you approach and tackle projects, adding value to your portfolio.

By following these steps, you can create a compelling portfolio that effectively showcases your skills and sets you apart from the competition, even if you're a new freelancer. Remember, your portfolio is an ongoing project – keep it updated with your latest work as you progress in your freelance career.

◈ **Real-Life Case Study:**

David, a freelance writer, included blog posts he wrote on sustainable living on his portfolio, even though they weren't client work. This targeted approach helped him land his first paying gig writing content for an eco-friendly clothing brand.

Step 3: Create a Competitive Profile on Freelance Platforms

Freelance platforms connect freelancers with potential clients. Utilize these platforms to market your services and find work opportunities.

Unveiling the Freelancing Landscape: A Guide

to Popular Platforms

FREELANCING PLATFORMS are the bustling marketplaces of the online working world. They connect freelancers with a vast pool of potential clients, streamlining the process of finding work and showcasing your skills.

Freelance Platforms: Utilize these platforms to market your services and find work opportunities. Research and choose platforms relevant to your niche. Some popular options include Upwork, a platform known for its wide range of freelance projects, and Fiverr, a platform known for offering micro-services. Craft compelling profiles that highlight your skills, experience, and unique selling proposition (USP). Set competitive rates based on your experience and the market value of your services.

Following is a breakdown of how to leverage these platforms to your advantage.

PLATFORM DIVERSITY: The freelancing landscape boasts a variety of platforms, each catering to specific niches and project types. Research and choose platforms that align with your skills and target audience.

Examples of Platforms by Niche:

Upwork: A broad platform encompassing a wide range of freelance projects, from writing and graphic design to programming and virtual assistance.

Fiverr: Known for its "micro-services" model, where freelancers offer smaller, well-defined services at set prices. Ideal for freelance writers, editors, and graphic designers offering specific package

Toptal: A high-end platform catering to elite freelancers in fields like software development, finance, and design. Requires a rigorous screening process to ensure top quality talent.

PeoplePerHour: A platform popular among freelancers in Europe and the UK, offering project-based and hourly work opportunities.

Freelancer.com: Another broad platform with a global reach, offering project listings across various creative and technical fields.

Optimizing Your Profile for Success:

ONCE YOU'VE CHOSEN your platform, create a compelling profile that grabs the attention of potential clients.

Headline & About Me: Craft a clear and concise headline that summarizes your skills and niche. In your "About Me" section, showcase your experience, highlight your unique selling proposition (USP), and convey your enthusiasm for your work.

Portfolio Power: Integrate your portfolio website or link to your online portfolio platforms like Behance or Dribbble. Let your work speak for itself!

Competitive Rates: Research the typical rates for your services within your chosen platform and niche. Set competitive rates that reflect your experience and value proposition.

Marketing yourself on the Platform: These platforms often have features to help you market yourself and find clients:

Project Applications: Actively browse project listings and submit compelling proposals that showcase your understanding of the client's needs and how you can deliver exceptional results.

Client Communication: Maintain clear and professional communication with potential clients. Respond promptly to inquiries, answer questions thoroughly, and be upfront about your rates and availability.

Building a Reputation: Deliver excellent service and exceed client expectations. Positive client reviews and testimonials will go a long way in building trust and attracting future projects.

Actionable Tip:

Research and choose platforms relevant to your niche.

Craft compelling profiles that highlight your skills, experience, and unique selling proposition (USP).

Set competitive rates based on your experience and the market value of your services.

By following these steps and strategically utilizing freelancing platforms, you can increase your visibility, connect with potential clients, and jumpstart your successful freelance career. Remember, it's not just about being on the platform – it's about actively engaging, showcasing your value, and building strong relationships with potential clients.

Real-Life Case Study:

After finalizing her niche, Sarah created profiles on Upwork and Fiverr showcasing her travel design portfolio and competitive rates. She also included positive client testimonials from previous freelance projects to build trust with potential clients.

Beyond the Basics:

Building a Sustainable Freelance Business

WHILE THESE STEPS GET you started, building a successful freelance business requires a long-term approach. Here are some additional tips:

◈ **Network and Build Relationships:** Connect with other freelancers and potential clients on social media and industry forums.

◈ **Develop a Client Acquisition Strategy:** Utilize a combination of freelance platforms, cold emailing, and social media marketing to find clients.

◈ **Deliver Excellent Client Service:** Prioritize communication, meet deadlines, and exceed client expectations to build a positive reputation and secure repeat business.

By following these steps and continuously honing your skills, you can turn freelancing into a thriving online business that offers freedom, flexibility, and financial rewards.

Unveiling the E-commerce Landscape

Your Guide to Selling Products Online

THE INTERNET HAS REVOLUTIONIZED commerce, opening doors for anyone with a product or service to reach a global audience. Whether you're a creative entrepreneur with handcrafted goods or a business-minded individual looking to source and resell products, the online world offers a plethora of options. Here, we'll delve into some popular methods for selling products online:

Dropshipping: A Low-Overhead Business Model

Dropshipping allows you to run an online store without managing physical inventory. Here's how it works:

You establish an online store: This is your virtual storefront where you showcase the products you'll be selling. Your online store is the cornerstone of your e-commerce journey. It's your virtual storefront, the platform where you'll showcase your products, entice customers, and convert them into paying patrons. Here's a breakdown of the steps involved in establishing your online store:

1. CHOOSING THE RIGHT E-commerce Platform:

This is a crucial decision, as your platform will determine the features available, ease of use, scalability, and overall functionality of your online store. Here are some factors to consider:

Your Technical Expertise: Are you comfortable with technology, or do you need a user-friendly platform with minimal technical requirements?

Your Budget: E-commerce platforms offer various pricing models, from freemium options with limited features to paid plans with extensive functionalities. Choose one that aligns with your budget and growth plans.

Features Needed: Consider the features essential for your online store, such as product management tools, payment processing options, marketing integrations, and inventory management tools.

Scalability: Think about your future plans. Will your product range and customer base expand over time? Choose a platform that can scale with your growing business.

Popular E-commerce Platforms

Shopify: A powerful and user-friendly platform with a comprehensive set of features, making it a great choice for businesses of all sizes.

Wix E-commerce: Offers ease of use and integrates seamlessly with the Wix website builder, ideal for beginners who already have a Wix website.

BigCommerce: A robust platform suitable for growing businesses with a large product catalog and complex needs.

Squarespace E-commerce: Known for its beautiful templates, Squarespace E-commerce provides a user-friendly platform for building stylish online stores.

WooCommerce (for WordPress): If you already have a WordPress website, consider WooCommerce, a popular plugin that transforms your WordPress site into a fully functional online store.

2. Selecting a Domain Name and Web Hosting:

Domain Name: This is your online store's address on the internet (e.g., yourstore.com). Choose a name that is memorable, reflects your brand, and is easy to spell and type. Many e-commerce platforms offer domain name registration services.

Web Hosting: This is where your online store's files and data reside. Reliable web hosting ensures your website is accessible to customers 24/7. Some e-commerce platforms include web hosting in their plans, while others require you to purchase it separately.

3. Designing and Building Your Online Store:

Choose a Theme: Many e-commerce platforms offer pre-designed themes that you can customize to match your brand identity. Prioritize a theme that is visually appealing, user-friendly for navigation, and optimized for mobile devices.

Product Listings and Descriptions: Create compelling product listings that showcase high-quality photos, detailed descriptions, and clear specifications. Highlight product features and benefits to entice customers.

Easy Navigation: Ensure your online store has a clear and intuitive navigation system. Customers should be able to find what they're looking for quickly and effortlessly.

Seamless Checkout Process: Offer a user-friendly checkout process with multiple secure payment options. Streamline the checkout process to minimize cart abandonment.

4. Adding Essential Features:

Payment Processing: Integrate secure payment gateways like PayPal, Stripe, or credit card processing to enable customers to make secure online purchases.

Shipping and Returns Policy: Clearly outline your shipping options, costs, and estimated delivery times. Establish a customer-friendly return policy to build trust.

Security Measures: Implement security measures like SSL certificates to encrypt customer data and ensure a secure shopping experience.

5. Launching Your Online Store and Beyond:

Test and Optimize: Before launching, thoroughly test all functionalities of your online store, ensuring a smooth shopping experience for customers.

Marketing and Promotion: Develop a marketing strategy to attract customers to your online store. Utilize social media marketing, search engine optimization (SEO), and other digital marketing channels to drive traffic and sales.

Analytics and Monitoring: Track key metrics like website traffic, conversion rates, and customer behaviour. Use this data to analyse your online store's performance and identify areas for improvement.

Remember: Building a successful online store is an ongoing process. By following these steps, you'll establish a solid foundation for your virtual storefront. Continuously learn, adapt, and refine your online store based on customer feedback and market trends to keep your business thriving in the ever-evolving world of e-commerce.

Partnering with a Dropshipping Supplier:

A Streamlined Approach to Fulfilling Orders

DROPSHIPPING offers a convenient and cost-effective way to sell products online without managing your own inventory. Here's a breakdown of how to partner with a dropshipping supplier:

1. Identifying the Right Dropshipping Supplier:

Research your Niche: The first step is to identify a profitable niche for your online store. This will determine the type of products you'll sell and the dropshipping suppliers you'll target.

Supplier Research and Evaluation: Once you've chosen your niche, research potential dropshipping suppliers. Look for suppliers with a good reputation, a wide range of products relevant to your niche, competitive pricing, and reliable shipping practices. Here are some resources to help you find dropshipping suppliers:

Online Directories: Platforms like SaleHoo, Doba, and Worldwide Brands list dropshipping suppliers across various categories. These directories often include supplier reviews and pricing information (may require a subscription fee).

Wholesale Websites: Many wholesalers also offer dropshipping services. Research wholesale websites related to your chosen niche to see if they dropship.

Manufacturer Websites: Some manufacturers may offer dropshipping programs directly. Check the websites of manufacturers of products you're interested in selling.

Evaluate Supplier Criteria: Don't just pick the first supplier you find. Carefully evaluate potential partners based on the following criteria:

Product Quality: Ensure the supplier offers high-quality products that align with your brand image and customer expectations. Request samples if possible to assess quality first-hand.

Pricing and Minimum Order Quantities (MOQs): Compare pricing across different suppliers and consider any minimum order quantities they might have.

Shipping and Fulfilment Times: Choose a supplier with reliable and efficient shipping practices. Consider factors like shipping costs, estimated delivery times, and whether they offer tracking information.

Customer Service: Partner with a dropshipping supplier with responsive and helpful customer service in case you encounter any issues.

2. Establishing a Partnership with the Dropshipping Supplier:

Contact the Supplier: Once you've identified a promising dropshipping supplier, reach out to them and inquire about their dropshipping program.

Review Dropshipping Agreement: Carefully review the supplier's dropshipping agreement. This document outlines the terms of your partnership, including pricing, shipping procedures, return policies, and any limitations.

Set up Your Online Store: While finalizing your dropshipping agreement, proceed with setting up your online store. List the products you'll be selling, ensuring product descriptions, images, and pricing are accurate and enticing to potential customers.

3. Processing Customer Orders and Fulfilment:

Customer Orders: Once you receive an order through your online store, forward the order details (including customer information and product specifications) to your dropshipping supplier.

Order Fulfilment: The dropshipping supplier will then process the order, package the products, and ship them directly to your customer under your brand name.

Customer Communication: Maintain clear communication with your customers throughout the order fulfilment process. Provide them with estimated delivery timelines and tracking information. Address any customer inquiries promptly and professionally.

4. Managing Your Dropshipping Business:

Inventory Management: While you won't physically hold inventory, it's crucial to stay updated on your dropshipping supplier's stock levels. Regularly check their inventory to avoid situations where you advertise out-of-stock products.

Marketing and Sales: Focus on marketing your online store and generating sales. Utilize various marketing strategies like search engine optimization (SEO), social media marketing, and email marketing to drive traffic to your store.

Customer Service: Provide excellent customer service to build trust and encourage repeat business. Address customer inquiries promptly and efficiently, even if issues pertain to fulfilment or product quality (handled by the dropshipping supplier).

Remember: Dropshipping can be a great way to start an online business with minimal upfront investment. However, it requires careful planning, selecting reliable suppliers, and focusing on marketing and customer service to succeed in the long run. Continuously monitor your dropshipping partnership, analyse your online store's performance, and adapt your strategies to optimize your e-commerce business.

Focus on marketing and customer service: Your responsibility lies in marketing your products, processing orders, and providing excellent customer service.

Pros:

Low upfront investment: No need to purchase inventory in bulk, minimizing financial risk.

Scalable business model: Easily add or remove products based on customer demand.

Location independence: Run your online store from anywhere with an internet connection.

Cons:

Lower profit margins: Dropshipping suppliers typically take a cut of the sale price.

Less control over product quality and shipping: You rely on the supplier to fulfill orders efficiently.

Potentially higher product pricing: Dropshipped products often have higher prices than those bought in bulk.

2. E-commerce Marketplaces: Reach a Built-in Audience

E-commerce marketplaces like Amazon, eBay, Etsy, and Walmart Marketplace already have a vast customer base, making them ideal platforms for new sellers.

E-commerce marketplaces offer a launch pad for new sellers, providing access to a vast customer base and established infrastructure. Here's a closer look at the merits of some leading marketplaces:

1. Amazon Marketplace: The E-commerce Behemoth

Pros:

Unmatched Customer Base: Boasts the largest online customer base globally, giving your products immense exposure.

Fulfilment by Amazon (FBA): Leverage Amazon's world-class fulfilment network for storage, packaging, and shipping (additional fees apply).

Brand Recognition and Trust: Customers inherently trust Amazon, potentially boosting conversions for your products.

Cons:

Cutthroat Competition: Millions of sellers vie for attention, making it challenging to stand out.

High Fees: Seller fees can add up quickly, including listing fees, referral fees, and storage fees for FBA.

Strict Regulations: Amazon has stringent product listing guidelines and performance metrics sellers must adhere to.

2. eBay: The Auction Powerhouse

Pros:

Auction Format: Ideal for selling unique or vintage items where bidding can drive up the price.

Global Reach: Attracts a diverse customer base from around the world.

Flexible Listing Options: Choose between auction-style listings or fixed-price formats.

Cons:

Declining User Base: While still significant, eBay's user base has shrunk compared to Amazon's growth.

Lower Average Order Value: Often associated with deals and used items, potentially leading to lower profits.

Higher Competition for Popular Products: Similar to Amazon, popular categories can be saturated with sellers.

3. Etsy: The Creative Crafter's Haven

Pros:

Targeted Audience: A dedicated marketplace for handmade, vintage, and craft supplies, attracting a passionate customer base.

Strong Community Focus: Etsy fosters a supportive community of sellers and buyers, ideal for fostering brand loyalty.

Lower Fees Compared to Amazon: Generally lower fees can be beneficial for sellers with smaller product catalogues.

Cons:

Limited Market Reach: Customer base is smaller compared to general e-commerce marketplaces.

Focus on Handmade Crafts: May not be suitable for all product types, especially mass-produced items.

Search Engine Optimization (SEO) Challenges: Standing out in search results can be more difficult on a niche platform.

4. Walmart Marketplace: The Rising Star

Pros:

Growing User Base: Walmart's online presence is rapidly expanding, offering access to a loyal customer base.

Competitive Fees: Generally lower fees compared to Amazon, potentially increasing profit margins.

Potential for Brand Recognition: Leverage Walmart's brand reputation to build trust with budget-conscious customers.

Cons:

Newer Platform: Less established seller tools and support systems compared to mature marketplaces.

Strict Seller Requirements: Qualifying to sell on Walmart Marketplace can be more challenging than other platforms.

Limited Product Categories: Currently, Walmart Marketplace focuses on specific product categories.

Choosing the Right Marketplace:

By understanding the strengths and weaknesses of each platform, you can make an informed decision about where to sell your products. Consider factors like your target audience, product type, budget, and growth goals. You can even leverage multiple marketplaces to reach a wider audience and diversify your sales channels.

◈ **Benefits:**

o Instant access to a large audience of potential buyers.

o Established infrastructure for payment processing and customer support.

o Often offer marketing and advertising tools to help you stand out.

◈ **Considerations:**

o Competition can be fierce, especially for popular products.

o Marketplace fees can eat into your profits.

o Less control over branding and customer experience.

Building Your Own E-commerce Empire

The Power and Responsibility of Owning Your Online Store

For entrepreneurs seeking complete autonomy and the ability to build a long-lasting brand presence, creating your own online store is the ultimate path. Here, you'll hold the reins on every aspect of the customer experience, from the initial storefront design to the post-purchase communication.

TAKING CONTROL OF YOUR Brand Identity:

Design Freedom: Craft a unique and visually appealing storefront that reflects your brand personality. You aren't limited to pre-designed templates found on marketplace platforms.

Content Strategy: Craft compelling product descriptions, blog posts, and marketing materials that resonate with your target audience and establish your brand voice.

Building Customer Loyalty: Direct customer relationships allow you to gather valuable feedback, implement loyalty programs, and foster a sense of community around your brand.

The Power of Customization:

Product Selection and Pricing: Complete control over your product curation allows you to offer unique items or bundles not available on marketplaces. You can also set competitive prices and implement strategic promotions.

Payment Processing: Choose a payment gateway that integrates seamlessly with your store and offers the features you need, such as recurring payments or subscriptions.

Marketing and Analytics: Utilize a variety of marketing tools and track website analytics to understand your audience, optimize your sales funnel, and refine your marketing campaigns.

Shouldering the Responsibility:

While the freedom of an independent store is empowering, it also comes with responsibilities:

Website Development and Maintenance: Choosing the right e-commerce platform (like Shopify or WooCommerce) and ensuring your store is user-friendly and mobile-optimized.

Choosing Your E-commerce Platform:

The Foundation of Your Online Store

The e-commerce platform you choose acts as the foundation for your online store. It will determine the functionalities, design flexibility, and overall user experience for both you (the store owner) and your customers. Here's a breakdown of key factors to consider when selecting the right platform:

1. EASE OF USE AND Scalability:

Shopify: Known for its user-friendly interface and intuitive setup process. Perfect for beginners with little technical knowledge. Offers a variety of add-on apps to enhance functionality as your store grows.

WooCommerce: A WordPress plugin, requiring some familiarity with WordPress installation and management. Offers a high degree of customization but can have a steeper learning curve for beginners.

2. Features and Functionality:

Built-in Features: Consider the features essential for your store, such as product management tools, inventory tracking, payment processing options, and built-in marketing functionalities. Evaluate which platform offers the features you need out-of-the-box, and how much you'd rely on additional extensions or plugins.

Scalability: Think about your long-term vision. Will your store offer a small product catalogue or a vast selection? Will you need functionalities like subscriptions or recurring billing? Choose a platform that can accommodate your growth and future needs.

3. Design and Customization:

Design Templates: Both Shopify and WooCommerce offer a variety of pre-designed themes that you can customize to match your brand identity. Shopify generally has a wider selection of user-friendly themes. WooCommerce offers more flexibility for advanced users to create a completely unique storefront design.

Mobile Optimization: In today's mobile-first world, ensure your chosen platform offers responsive themes or built-in mobile optimization tools. Your store should display flawlessly and be user-friendly on all devices (desktops, tablets, and smartphones).

4. Pricing and Transaction Fees:

Subscription Fees: Both platforms have monthly subscription plans with varying pricing tiers. Choose a plan that aligns with your store's size and transaction volume.

Transaction Fees: Some platforms charge additional transaction fees on each sale. Factor these fees into your pricing strategy to maintain profitability.

5. App Integrations and Ecosystem:

- **App Stores:** Both Shopify and WooCommerce offer app stores with a vast selection of extensions and plugins. These can add functionalities like advanced marketing tools, loyalty programs, shipping integrations, and more. Consider the available apps and their costs when making your decision.

Additional Considerations:

- **Security:** Choose a platform with robust security features to protect your customer data and ensure a safe shopping experience.
- **Payment Processing Options:** Ensure the platform integrates with popular payment gateways to offer your customers convenient payment options.
- **Customer Support:** Reliable customer support is crucial in case you encounter technical difficulties. Evaluate the quality and availability of support offered by each platform.

Inventory Management: Implementing a robust system for tracking stock levels, managing orders, and ensuring smooth fulfilment.

Conquering the Chaos: Mastering Inventory Management for Your Online Store. Inventory management is the lifeblood of any successful e-commerce business. It ensures you have the right products in stock to fulfil customer orders while minimizing the risk of overstocking or running out of popular items. Here's a

breakdown of key strategies to implement a robust inventory management system for your online store:

1. CHOOSING THE RIGHT Inventory Management System:

◈ **Manual System (For Starters):** For stores with a limited product catalogue, a simple spreadsheet might suffice initially. Track stock levels, record incoming and outgoing inventory, and set reorder points to avoid stockouts.

◈ **Inventory Management Software:** As your store grows, consider investing in dedicated inventory management software. These programs automate many tasks, offer real-time inventory tracking, generate purchase orders, and integrate with your e-commerce platform.

2. Implementing Accurate Stock Tracking:

◈ **Regular Stock Counts:** Conduct periodic physical inventory checks to ensure your system's data aligns with the actual stock levels.

◈ **Accounting for Stock Movement:** Track all inventory movements – incoming shipments, sales, returns, damages, and samples.

◈ **SKU Management:** Assign a unique SKU (Stock Keeping Unit) code to each product variation (size, colour, etc.) for efficient identification and tracking.

3. Setting Reorder Points and Lead Times:

◇ **Reorder Point:** The stock level at which you need to place a new order to avoid stockouts. This factors in average sales velocity, lead times (time it takes to receive new inventory), and safety stock buffer.

◇ **Lead Times:** Understand the lead times for your suppliers to ensure you order new inventory well in advance to avoid stockouts. Factor in potential delays during peak seasons or unexpected situations.

4. Managing Stock Levels and Product Assortment:

◇ **ABC Analysis:** Prioritize inventory management efforts by categorizing products based on their sales volume and profitability. Focus on closely monitoring and optimizing stock levels for your high-selling (A category) and moderately selling (B category) products.

◇ **Slow-Moving Inventory:** Develop strategies to deal with slow-moving inventory, such as offering discounts, bundling them with popular products, or running clearance sales.

5. Optimizing Fulfilment for a Seamless Customer Experience:

◇ **Pick and Pack Efficiency:** Streamline your order fulfilment process to minimize picking and packing errors and ensure timely order shipments.

◇ **Shipping Integration:** Integrate your inventory management system with your chosen shipping carriers for faster and more accurate order fulfilment.

◇ **Real-Time Inventory Updates:** Update your online store's inventory levels in real-time to avoid customer frustration due to inaccurate product availability information.

By implementing these strategies and tailoring them to your specific business needs, you can establish a robust inventory management system that keeps your online store running smoothly, minimizes stock outs, and optimizes your cash flow. By carefully considering these factors and researching the specific functionalities offered by Shopify and WooCommerce, you can choose the platform that best suits your needs and sets your online store up for success. Remember, the ideal platform should empower you to build a user-friendly, visually appealing, and mobile-optimized store that converts visitors into customers.

Mastering the Customer Magnet:

UNVEILING MARKETING Strategies for Your Online Store. In the vast e-commerce landscape, a beautiful online store alone isn't enough. To thrive, you need to attract potential customers and convert them into loyal buyers. Here's a breakdown of key marketing strategies to drive traffic to your store, acquire new customers, and build a thriving online presence:

1. Search Engine Optimization (SEO): The Organic Powerhouse

◈ **Keyword Research:** Identify relevant keywords that potential customers use to search for products like yours. Optimize your product listings, website content, and Meta descriptions with these keywords to improve your organic ranking on search engines like Google.

◈ **Content Marketing:** Create valuable and informative content related to your products and target audience. This could include blog posts, buying guides, how-to articles, or info graphics. High-quality content establishes you as an authority, attracts organic traffic, and improves SEO ranking.

◈ **Technical SEO:** Ensure your website is mobile-friendly, has fast loading times, and implements best practices for technical SEO to improve search engine visibility.

2. Social Media Marketing: Building Brand Awareness and Engagement

◈ **Identify Your Target Platforms:** Choose the social media platforms where your target audience spends their time. Focus your efforts on those platforms to maximize reach and engagement.

◇ **Compelling Content is Key:** Create engaging social media content that showcases your products, highlights brand values, and fosters interaction with your audience. Utilize high-quality visuals, run contests or giveaways, and respond promptly to comments and messages.

◇ **Leverage Influencer Marketing:** Partner with relevant social media influencers in your niche to promote your products to their audience. This can be a powerful strategy to gain brand exposure and reach a wider audience.

3. Pay-Per-Click (PPC) Advertising: Targeted Traffic Acquisition

◇ **Platform Options:** Consider advertising on search engines like Google Ads or social media platforms like Facebook Ads. These platforms allow you to create targeted campaigns based on demographics, interests, and online behaviour.

◇ **Campaign Optimization:** Track your PPC campaign performance closely, analyse data, and optimize your campaigns to maximize return on investment (ROI).

4. Email Marketing: Building Relationships and Fostering Loyalty

◇ **Building an Email List:** Encourage visitors to subscribe to your email list by offering incentives like discounts or exclusive content.

◇ **Nurture Leads with Email Campaigns:** Create targeted email campaigns to educate potential customers about your products, offer promotions, and drive sales.

◇ **Segmentation:** Segment your email list based on customer preferences and purchase history to send more relevant and personalized emails that resonate better.

5. Content Marketing and Public Relations:

◈ **Guest Blogging:** Contribute guest blog posts on relevant industry websites to reach a wider audience and establish yourself as an expert.

◈ **Online Reviews and Reputation Management:** Encourage satisfied customers to leave positive reviews on your website and other online platforms. Proactively address negative reviews and demonstrate excellent customer service.

Remember, a successful marketing strategy is multifaceted. Combine these strategies, track your results, and adapt your approach based on what resonates most with your target audience. The key is to consistently provide value, build trust, and convert website visitors into loyal customers who keep coming back for more.

Building a Customer-Centric Brand: The Heart of E-commerce Success

◈ **Customer Service:** Providing excellent customer service is crucial for building trust and repeat business. You'll be responsible for handling inquiries, resolving issues, and ensuring customer satisfaction. While effective marketing strategies attract customers to your online store, fostering a customer-centric brand is what keeps them coming back for more. Here's how to cultivate a brand identity that prioritizes customer satisfaction and builds long-term loyalty:

1. Prioritize Exceptional Customer Service:

◇ **Prompt and Professional Support:** Offer multiple channels for customer support, such as live chat, email, and phone. Ensure prompt responses from a knowledgeable and friendly support team.

◇ **Going the Extra Mile:** Exceed customer expectations whenever possible. Offer solutions that go beyond the bare minimum to build trust and foster loyalty.

◇ **Proactive Communication:** Keep customers informed about order status, potential delays, and any relevant updates. Transparency builds trust and reduces customer frustration.

2. Cultivating a Community around Your Brand

◇ **Social Media Interaction:** Actively engage with your audience on social media platforms. Respond to comments, answer questions, and participate in relevant conversations.

◇ **Loyalty Programs:** Reward repeat customers with loyalty programs that offer exclusive discounts, early access to sales, or other perks. This incentivizes repeat business and strengthens customer relationships.

◇ **Customer Reviews and Testimonials:** Encourage customer reviews on your website and other online platforms. Positive testimonials act as social proof and build trust with potential customers.

3. The Power of User-Generated Content (UGC):

◇ **Customer Showcase:** Encourage customers to share photos and videos using your products on social media with a branded hashtag. UGC is a powerful marketing tool that leverages customer enthusiasm and authenticity.

◈ **Contests and Giveaways:** Run contests and giveaways that encourage user-generated content related to your brand. This is a fun way to increase brand awareness, generate excitement, and engage your audience.

4. Prioritize Personalization and Recommendations:

◈ **Product Recommendations:** Utilize website analytics and customer data to recommend products that are relevant to past purchases or browsing behaviour. Personalization enhances the customer experience and increases the chance of conversions.

◈ **Targeted Email Campaigns:** Segment your email list based on customer preferences and purchase history. Send personalized emails with product recommendations, special offers, and content that resonates with individual customer needs.

5. Embrace Feedback and Continuous Improvement:

◈ **Customer Surveys and Feedback Forms:** Regularly collect customer feedback through surveys and feedback forms. Actively listen to their suggestions and concerns.

◈ **Data-Driven Decisions:** Analyse customer data, website traffic patterns, and sales trends to identify areas for improvement and optimize your online store based on customer behaviour.

By prioritizing customer satisfaction and building a brand that resonates with your target audience, you can create a thriving online store that fosters customer loyalty and drives long-term success. Remember, in the e-commerce landscape, exceptional customer service and a commitment to building relationships are just as important as eye-catching marketing campaigns.

Is Building Your Own Store Right for You?

OWNING YOUR ONLINE store is a rewarding path for those who crave complete control and a long-term brand-building strategy. However, it requires a significant investment of time, effort, and potentially resources compared to selling on established marketplaces. Carefully consider your resources, technical skills, and long-term goals before embarking on this path. You can always start by testing the waters on a marketplace and then migrate to your own store once you've established a customer base and brand identity.

◇ **Pros:**

o Full control over branding and customer experience.

o Greater profit margins compared to dropshipping or marketplaces.

o Ability to build long-term customer relationships and loyalty.

◇ **Cons:**

o Higher upfront investment: Requires setting up the store, managing inventory, and potentially marketing efforts.

o Attracting customers can be challenging initially.

o Greater responsibility for customer service and order fulfillment.

Choosing the Right Path:

The best method for selling products online depends on your resources, risk tolerance, and long-term goals. Consider the following factors:

◇ **Start-up costs:** How much can you invest upfront in inventory or website development?

◇ **Product type:** Is your product well-suited for drop shipping or handmade marketplaces?

◇ **Time commitment:** Are you prepared to manage inventory and customer service, or do you prefer a more hands-off approach?

By carefully considering these factors and exploring the options available, you can choose the e-commerce path that best suits your needs and sets you on the road to online sales success.

Content Creation Powerhouse:

Building an Audience and Monetizing Your Expertise

CONTENT CREATION IS a cornerstone of modern marketing, allowing you to establish yourself as an authority, attract a loyal audience, and unlock various revenue streams. Here's a breakdown of how to leverage content creation to build a following and monetize your efforts:

1. Choosing Your Content Playground:

◈ **Blogging:** Perfect for in-depth articles, tutorials, and long-form content. Offers flexibility in terms of topics and allows for integration with your online store.

Unveiling the Power of Blogging

A CONTENT MARKETING Powerhouse for E-commerce. Blogging sits at the heart of many successful e-commerce content creation strategies. Its versatility allows you to delve into detailed product information, craft engaging tutorials, and establish yourself as an authority in your niche. Here's a closer look at the advantages blogging offers for e-commerce businesses:

Content Depth and Value:

◈ **In-Depth Product Information:** Blogs are ideal for providing comprehensive descriptions of your products. Go beyond basic specifications and highlight the features, benefits, and unique selling propositions (USPs) that set your products apart.

◈ **Detailed Tutorials and How-To Guides:** Educate your audience on how to use your products to their full potential. Step-by-step tutorials with clear instructions and high-quality visuals can significantly enhance the customer experience and encourage informed purchasing decisions.

◈ **Industry Insights and Trend Spotting:** Position yourself as a thought leader by sharing industry insights, analysing trends, and offering valuable commentary on topics relevant to your target audience.

SEO Optimization and Organic Traffic:

◈ **Keyword Targeting:** Optimize your blog posts for relevant keywords that potential customers might use when searching for products like yours. This strategy increases your website's visibility in search engine results pages (SERPs) and drives organic traffic to your online store.

◈ **Content Hub:** A well-maintained blog acts as a content hub, attracting visitors through informative and engaging posts. This not only increases brand awareness but also positions you as a resource for valuable information, fostering trust and credibility with potential customers.

◈ **Long-Term Content Value:** Unlike social media posts that fade quickly, well-researched and informative blog content has a longer lifespan. Optimized blog posts can continue to attract organic traffic for months or even years to come.

Integration with Your Online Store:

◇ **Product Reviews and Comparisons:** Write in-depth product reviews, comparing your offerings to competitor products. Highlight the advantages of your products and showcase their value proposition.

◇ **Targeted Calls to Action (CTAs):** Strategically integrate CTAs within your blog posts. Direct readers to relevant product pages, encourage them to subscribe to your email list, or offer exclusive discounts for blog readers.

◇ **Building Customer Relationships:** Blogs foster a more personal connection with your audience. Respond to comments, address questions, and engage in discussions to build trust and loyalty.

Additional Considerations:

◇ **Content Calendar and Consistency:** Maintaining a consistent publishing schedule is crucial. Develop a content calendar to plan topics, research keywords, and ensure a steady flow of high-quality blog posts.

◇ **Visual Appeal:** Complement your text with high-quality images, infographics, and videos to enhance reader engagement and break up long blocks of text.

◇ **Content Promotion:** Promote your blog posts on social media platforms, relevant online communities, and through email marketing to maximize reach and attract new readers.

By leveraging the power of blogging, you can create valuable content that educates your audience, drives organic traffic to your online store, and ultimately converts visitors into loyal customers. Remember, a well-maintained blog is a powerful tool for building brand awareness, establishing expertise, and achieving long-term success in the ever-evolving e-commerce landscape.

Building a Thriving E-commerce YouTube Channel

⬦ **YouTube Channel:** Ideal for visual learners and product demonstrations. Leverage video content to showcase your personality, engage your audience, and create a more immersive experience. In today's visually driven world, YouTube presents a powerful platform for e-commerce businesses. By creating engaging video content, you can showcase your products, connect with your audience on a personal level, and drive sales to your online store. Here's a breakdown of the key advantages YouTube offers for e-commerce businesses:

VISUAL STORYTELLING and Product Demonstrations:

⬦ **Show, Don't Tell:** Captivate your audience with visually appealing demonstrations of your products. Highlight features, benefits, and functionalities in a way that static images or text descriptions simply can't.

⬦ **Unboxing Videos and Customer Reviews:** Partner with influencers or loyal customers to create unboxing videos that generate excitement around your products. Customer testimonials build trust and social proof, influencing purchasing decisions.

⬦ **Live Q&A Sessions and Product Launches:** Host live Q&A sessions to interact directly with your audience, answer their questions, and build a sense of community. Use live streams to launch new products and create a buzz around your brand.

Building Brand Personality and Audience Engagement:

◈ **Leverage Your Personality:** Let your personality shine through in your videos. Your enthusiasm and passion for your products will resonate with viewers and create a more personal connection.

◈ **Storytelling and Entertainment:** Don't just focus on selling. Craft engaging video narratives that entertain your audience while subtly showcasing your products. Humor, informative storytelling, and behind-the-scenes glimpses can be powerful tools for engagement.

◈ **Community Building:** Encourage viewers to subscribe to your channel, like your videos, and leave comments. Respond to comments, host contests, and foster a sense of community around your brand.

Driving Sales and Conversions:

◈ **Strategic CTAs:** Integrate clear calls to action (CTAs) within your videos. Direct viewers to your online store, encourage them to subscribe for more content, or offer exclusive discounts for YouTube viewers.

◈ **Product Links in Video Descriptions:** Include links to relevant product pages in your video descriptions. Make it easy for viewers to learn more and purchase the products they see in action.

◇ **Leverage YouTube Ads:** Utilize targeted YouTube ads to reach a wider audience and promote specific products or special offers relevant to your target demographics.

Optimizing Your YouTube Channel for Success:

◈ **SEO Optimization:** Optimize your video titles, descriptions, and tags with relevant keywords to improve search engine ranking and discoverability on YouTube.

◈ **High-Quality Production:** While fancy equipment isn't essential, strive for clear audio, good lighting, and engaging visuals. A professional presentation enhances the viewing experience and reflects positively on your brand.

◈ **Consistency is Key:** Develop a consistent upload schedule to keep your audience engaged. Publish new videos regularly to maintain momentum and build anticipation.

◈ **Analytics and Data Tracking:** Utilize YouTube analytics to track video performance, understand audience demographics, and identify areas for improvement.

BY CREATING INFORMATIVE, entertaining, and visually appealing video content, you can leverage the power of YouTube to build brand awareness, engage your target audience, and ultimately drive sales for your e-commerce business. Remember, consistency, audience interaction, and strategic optimization are key to building a thriving YouTube channel that fuels your e-commerce success.

Building an E-commerce Podcast That Captivates

⟡ **Podcasts:** Excellent for niche topics, in-depth discussions, and interviews with industry experts. Podcasts offer a convenient format for listeners to consume content on the go.

WHILE IMAGES REIGN supreme on YouTube, the power of audio storytelling shouldn't be underestimated. Podcasts offer a unique opportunity to connect with your audience on a deeper level, establish yourself as an industry expert, and ultimately drive sales for your e-commerce business. Here's a breakdown of the unique advantages podcasts offer for e-commerce ventures:

In-Depth Discussions and Industry Insights:

⟡ **Niche-Specific Topics:** Delve into topics relevant to your niche with in-depth discussions, interviews with industry experts, and product analyses. Offer valuable insights that educate your audience and position you as a thought leader.

⟡ **Problem-solving Focus:** Podcasts allow for a more conversational format, ideal for tackling customer pain points, offering solutions, and showcasing how your products can address specific challenges.

⟡ **Building Trust through Authenticity:** The audio format fosters a sense of intimacy, allowing you to connect with listeners on a personal level and build trust through genuine conversations.

Targeted Audience Engagement and Community Building:

◈ **Niche Communities:** Podcasts cater to specific interests, allowing you to target a highly engaged audience with whom you share a common passion. Build a community around your podcast by encouraging listener interaction.

◈ **Call to Actions (CTAs) with Context:** Integrate CTAs seamlessly within your podcast discussions. Recommend relevant products or services within the context of the conversation, making them more likely to resonate with listeners.

◈ **Listener Interaction and Feedback:** Encourage listeners to interact by offering email addresses, social media handles, or even dedicated listener hotlines. Address their questions and concerns directly on future episodes, fostering a sense of community.

Content Versatility and Repurposing Opportunities:

◈ **Episode Formats:** Explore different episode formats like interviews, solo discussions, listener Q&A sessions, or even product reviews. This variety keeps your content fresh and caters to different listener preferences.

◈ **Content Repurposing:** Expand the reach of your podcast content by repurposing snippets into social media posts, blog articles, or short video clips. This maximizes the value you extract from your podcast episodes.

◇ **Leveraging Guest Appearances:** Appear as a guest on other relevant podcasts in your niche. This expands your reach and exposes you to a new audience, potentially driving traffic back to your online store.

Building Brand Awareness and Long-Term Growth:

◈ **Subscription Model and Recurring Listeners:** Encourage listeners to subscribe to your podcast on their preferred platforms. Building a loyal listener base ensures consistent engagement and a dedicated audience for your content.

◈ **Brand Storytelling:** Weave your brand story into the narrative of your podcast. Highlight the values and mission behind your business, fostering a deeper connection with listeners who resonate with your brand identity.

◈ **Long-Term Play:** Podcasts are a marathon, not a sprint. Building a successful podcast takes time and consistent effort. Focus on creating valuable content, engaging with your audience, and continuously adapting your strategy based on listener feedback.

BY HARNESSING THE POWER of audio storytelling, podcasts can be a valuable tool for e-commerce businesses. They allow you to connect with a targeted audience, establish industry expertise, and ultimately drive sales through well-placed CTAs and a focus on solving customer problems. Remember, consistency, audience engagement, and a commitment to delivering valuable content are key to building a thriving podcast that fuels the growth of your online store.

2. Identifying Your Niche and Target Audience:

◈ **Focus on Your Passion:** Choose a niche you're genuinely enthusiastic about. Your passion will translate into engaging content and keep you motivated over the long term.

◈ **Audience Persona:** Develop a clear understanding of your ideal audience. Research their demographics, interests, and pain points. Tailor your content to address their specific needs and challenges.

3. Content Strategy and Consistency:

◈ **Value-Driven Content:** Create informative and valuable content that solves problems, educates your audience, and entertains them. Consistency is key – establish a regular publishing schedule to keep your audience engaged.

◈ **SEO Optimization:** Optimize your content (blogs and website copy) for search engines to improve organic traffic and reach a wider audience.

◈ **Cross-Promotion:** Promote your content across different channels – share blog posts on social media, mention your podcast on your YouTube channel, and vice versa.

4. Building an Audience and Community:

◈ **Social Media Engagement:** Actively engage with your audience on social media platforms. Respond to comments, participate in relevant discussions, and run contests to build a community around your brand.

◈ **Guest Posting and Collaborations:** Collaborate with other creators in your niche by guest posting on their blogs or co-hosting episodes on their podcasts. This expands your reach and exposes you to new audiences.

◈ **Email Marketing:** Build an email list and nurture leads with targeted email campaigns that promote your content and special offers.

5. Unveiling the Monetization Strategies:

◈ **Advertising:** Once you've built a sizeable audience, you can display ads on your website or YouTube channel, generating revenue based on clicks or impressions.

Unveiling the Advertising Powerhouse:

Monetizing Your Audience through Strategic Ad Placement

ONCE YOU'VE CULTIVATED a sizeable audience through captivating content, engaging marketing strategies, or a combination of both, you can unlock a powerful revenue stream: advertising. Let's delve into the various advertising options available and explore how to integrate them for maximum impact without compromising the user experience:

1. Choosing the Right Advertising Model:

- **Cost-per-Thousand Impressions (CPM):** Earn revenue based on the number of times your ad is displayed (impressions), regardless of whether users click on it. This model is ideal for building brand awareness and reaching a large audience.
- **Cost-per-Click (CPC):** Earn revenue each time a user clicks on your ad. This model is effective for driving targeted traffic to your website or landing pages and potentially generating leads or sales.

2. Selecting the Optimal Ad Format:

- **Display Ads:** These visual ads come in various sizes (banners, rectangles, skyscrapers) and can be strategically placed on your website or YouTube channel. Display ads can showcase images, text, or even short animations to grab user attention.
- **Native Ads:** Designed to seamlessly blend with your website's content, native ads can be highly effective. They often take

the form of sponsored content or in-feed video ads that don't disrupt the user experience.

- **Video Ads:** With the rise of video consumption, pre-roll, mid-roll, and post-roll ads are popular on YouTube and other video platforms. These ads can be concise and visually engaging, showcasing product features or brand messages.

3. Targeting Your Audience with Precision:

- **Demographic Targeting:** Target your ads based on user demographics such as age, location, gender, income, and interests. This allows you to deliver highly relevant ads that resonate with specific audience segments.
- **Behavioural Targeting:** Leverage user behaviour data to display ads related to past website visits, search queries, or purchases. This ensures contextually relevant ads that are more likely to convert.
- **Retargeting:** Reconnect with website visitors who have already shown interest in your products or services. Retargeting campaigns can be highly successful in capturing previously lost leads and converting them into paying customers.

4. Tracking Performance and Optimization:

- **Analytics and Data Insights:** Utilize analytics tools provided by ad platforms to track ad performance, such as impressions, click-through rates (CTRs), and conversion rates.
- **A/B Testing:** Experiment with different ad formats, placements, and targeting strategies to see what resonates best with your audience. A/B testing helps you optimize your ad

campaigns for maximum return on investment (ROI).

- **Maintaining User Experience:** Always prioritize user experience. Strike a balance between generating revenue through advertising and ensuring a clean, user-friendly website or YouTube channel that doesn't overwhelm viewers with excessive ads.

By strategically integrating advertising, you can turn your online platform into a revenue-generating machine. Remember, the key lies in understanding your audience, selecting the right ad formats and targeting options, and constantly monitoring and optimizing your campaigns for the best results.

Additionally, consider these advanced advertising options to further monetize your audience:

- **Affiliate Marketing:** Partner with other businesses in your niche and promote their products or services. Earn a commission on every sale generated through your unique affiliate link.
- **Sponsorships:** Collaborate with relevant brands or influencers to sponsor your content or events. This allows you to leverage their audience reach while promoting their products or services.
- **Selling Premium Content:** Offer exclusive content, such as in-depth tutorials or membership programs, accessible only through paid subscriptions. This can be a valuable revenue stream for loyal audience members seeking premium value.

Unveiling the Power of Affiliate Marketing for E-commerce Businesses

◇ **Affiliate Marketing:** Promote other companies' products or services relevant to your niche. Earn a commission on every sale generated through your unique affiliate link. Affiliate marketing offers a compelling revenue stream for e-commerce businesses. It allows you to leverage the promotional power of others while focusing on building your own audience and brand. Here's a deeper look at how affiliate marketing works and how you can integrate it strategically into your overall marketing strategy:

UNDERSTANDING THE AFFILIATE Marketing Ecosystem:

◇ **The Players:** Three key players are involved – the merchant (company offering the product/service), the affiliate (you promoting the product/service), and the customer (who makes the purchase).

◇ **Earning Commissions:** You promote the merchant's product using a unique affiliate link. When a customer clicks on your link and completes a purchase, you earn a commission from the merchant.

Choosing the Right Affiliate Programs:

◇ **Relevance is Key:** Select affiliate programs that offer products or services relevant to your niche and target audience. Promoting products your audience genuinely needs or desires increases the chance of successful conversions.

◈ **Commission Structure:** Affiliate programs offer various commission structures, such as a percentage of the sale price, a fixed amount per sale, or even a commission for leads generated. Choose a program that aligns with your goals and provides a healthy incentive.

◈ **Program Reputation:** Research the reputation of the affiliate program and the merchant. Partner with trustworthy companies with a good track record of customer satisfaction and timely payouts to affiliates.

Promoting Affiliate Products Effectively:

◈ **Content Integration:** Seamlessly integrate affiliate links within your existing content – blog posts, YouTube videos, social media descriptions, or even podcast discussions. Provide valuable information and reviews on the product before directing users to the affiliate link.

◈ **Transparency is Essential:** Disclose that you're using affiliate links and explain how it benefits your audience. Transparency builds trust and encourages viewers/readers to click on your links with confidence.

◈ **Targeted Calls to Action (CTAs):** Don't leave your audience guessing. Include clear CTAs that encourage users to click on your affiliate links, whether it's visiting the merchant's website, checking out a specific product, or taking advantage of a limited-time offer.

Tracking Performance and Optimizing Strategies:

◇ **Affiliate Marketing Tools:** Utilize tools provided by affiliate programs to track clicks, conversions, and commission earned. Analyse this data to understand which products or promotional methods resonate best with your audience.

◇ **Content Performance:** Monitor which types of content (blog posts, videos, etc.) generate the most affiliate clicks and conversions. Focus on creating more content that performs well and adjust your strategy accordingly.

◇ **Building Long-Term Relationships:** Nurturing positive relationships with affiliate program managers can be beneficial. They might offer valuable insights, promotional resources, or exclusive deals you can leverage to boost your affiliate marketing success.

Remember, affiliate marketing is a collaborative effort. By choosing the right partners, promoting relevant products effectively, and continuously optimizing your strategies, you can use affiliate marketing as a powerful tool to generate additional revenue streams and fuel the growth of your e-commerce business.

Beyond the Basics:

Advanced Affiliate Marketing Strategies:

◇ **Coupon Codes and Exclusive Offers:** Partner with merchants to offer exclusive discounts or coupon codes to your audience. This incentivizes clicks and conversions while giving your audience a perceived advantage.

The Coupon Code Craze: Unleashing the Power of Exclusive Offers in E-commerce

COUPON CODES AND EXCLUSIVE offers are like magic words in the e-commerce world. They have the undeniable power to entice customers, boost conversions, and elevate your brand as a savvy deal provider. Here's a detailed exploration of how to leverage coupon codes and exclusive offers to supercharge your e-commerce marketing strategy:

Crafting Compelling Coupon Code Campaigns:

◇ **Know Your Audience:** Tailor your offers to resonate with your target audience. Consider demographics, buying habits, and what motivates them to purchase. For budget-conscious customers, a high-value discount code might be most appealing. For those seeking premium experiences, exclusive early access to new products could be the key.

◇ **Strike a Balance:** While discounts are attractive, avoid devaluing your brand with excessively deep cuts. Offer codes that incentivize purchases without sacrificing your profit margins. Consider offering free shipping or bundled product discounts instead of straight percentage reductions.

◇ **Time-Bound Exclusivity:** Create a sense of urgency by attaching deadlines to your coupon codes. This encourages immediate action and prevents customers from waiting for a potentially better deal later. However, avoid excessively short expiration periods that frustrate customers.

Strategic Partnerships for Broader Reach:

◇ **Collaborate with Influencers:** Partner with social media influencers or bloggers in your niche. Offer them exclusive coupon codes to promote to their audience. This leverages their influence and expands your reach to a targeted customer base.

◇ **Affiliate Marketing Integration:** Enhance your affiliate marketing efforts by providing affiliates with exclusive coupon codes to share with their audience. This incentivizes clicks on their affiliate links and increases the likelihood of conversions for both you and the affiliate.

◇ **Co-marketing Opportunities:** Partner with complementary businesses to offer bundled discounts or joint promotions. This strategy taps into each other's customer base and expands your reach to a wider audience.

Promoting Your Exclusive Offers Effectively:

◈ **Multi-Channel Marketing:** Announce your coupon codes across various channels – email marketing campaigns, social media posts, website banners, and even blog content.

◈ **Clear Communication:** Ensure your coupon codes are easy to find and understand. Clearly communicate the terms and conditions associated with each offer, including product eligibility, minimum purchase requirements, and expiration dates.

◈ **Scarcity and Urgency:** Create a sense of urgency by highlighting limited quantities or time-bound offers. Use phrases like "limited-time offer" or "while supplies last" to encourage immediate action from potential customers.

TRACKING PERFORMANCE and Optimizing Strategies:

◈ **Track Coupon Code Usage:** Monitor which coupons are being used most frequently and on what products. This data provides valuable insights into customer preferences and buying behavior.

◈ **A/B Testing:** Test different discount percentages, code expiration times, and promotional messages to see what resonates best with your audience. A/B testing helps you optimize your coupon code campaigns for maximum impact.

◈ **Post-Campaign Analysis:** Once a campaign ends, analyse the results. Measure the impact on sales, customer acquisition costs, and overall return on investment (ROI). Use this data to refine your future coupon code strategies for even better results.

By strategically implementing coupon codes and exclusive offers, you can transform them from a simple discount tactic into a powerful marketing tool. Remember, the key lies in understanding your audience, crafting compelling offers, and promoting them effectively across various channels. With a data-driven approach and continuous optimization, you can leverage the magic of coupon codes to drive sales, build brand loyalty, and propel your e-commerce business to new heights.

Crafting Compelling Product Comparisons to Drive Affiliate Sales

Product Comparisons and Reviews: Create comprehensive product comparisons and reviews that highlight the strengths and weaknesses of various products in your niche. Include your affiliate link for the product you recommend most highly.

IN TODAY'S INFORMATION-driven marketplace, consumers rely heavily on product reviews before making purchase decisions. Leveraging this trend, you can create comprehensive product comparisons and reviews that not only establish you as an authority in your niche but also drive affiliate sales through strategic recommendations. Here's a breakdown of what goes into crafting compelling product comparisons that convert:

Choosing Products for Comparison:

◈ **Relevance to Your Niche:** Focus on comparing products that are directly relevant to your target audience and niche. This ensures your audience finds the comparison genuinely informative and valuable.

◈ **Popularity and Emerging Trends:** Include popular products within your niche, alongside any emerging trends or new releases that might pique audience interest. Offer fresh perspectives on established products and educate viewers/readers about the latest innovations.

◈ **Competitor Analysis:** Compare your affiliate product with its main competitors in the market. Highlight the strengths and weaknesses of each product to provide a balanced and objective perspective.

Crafting Informative and Engaging Content:

◈ **In-Depth Analysis:** Go beyond simple product descriptions. Dive deeper into technical specifications, features, functionalities, and user experience.

◈ **Visual Appeal:** Complement your text with high-quality images, infographics, or even video demonstrations to enhance the user experience and break down complex information into easily digestible formats.

◈ **Clear Comparisons:** Utilize tables, charts, or side-by-side comparisons to showcase key differences between products. This allows viewers/readers to quickly identify the strengths and weaknesses of each contender.

Strategically Highlighting Your Affiliate Product:

◈ **Transparency and Credibility:** Disclose that you're using affiliate links and explain the benefits to your audience. Transparency builds trust and encourages them to consider your recommendations more seriously.

◈ **Highlighting Strengths:** Focus on the aspects where your affiliate product shines. Demonstrate how it addresses customer pain points more effectively than competitors, or how it offers unique features that set it apart.

◈ **Balanced Approach:** While showcasing the strengths of your affiliate product, maintain objectivity. Acknowledge potential drawbacks or limitations, allowing viewers/readers to make informed decisions based on all available information.

Call to Action and Conversion Optimization:

◈ **Strategic Placement of Affiliate Links:** Place your affiliate link prominently within your product comparison content. Consider including it within the product description, comparison table, or even within a clear call to action (CTA) at the end of your review.

◈ **Limited-Time Offers or Exclusive Discounts:** Partner with the merchant to offer exclusive discounts or limited-time deals to your audience. This incentivizes clicks on your affiliate link and increases the likelihood of conversions.

◈ **Addressing Purchase Concerns:** Anticipate any potential purchase roadblocks. Address common customer concerns, such as return policies, warranty information, or shipping costs. Providing comprehensive information increases trust and removes barriers to purchase.

TRACKING PERFORMANCE and Refinement:

◈ **Affiliate Marketing Tools:** Utilize tracking tools to monitor clicks, conversions, and revenue generated through your affiliate link for each product comparison.

◈ **Data-Driven Decisions:** Analyse data to identify which products or comparison formats resonate best with your audience. Focus on creating similar comparisons for products that generate high click-through and conversion rates.

◈ **Customer Feedback:** Encourage viewers/readers to leave comments and feedback on your product comparisons. Incorporate their questions and concerns into future reviews to continuously improve the value you deliver to your audience.

By crafting informative, engaging, and strategically optimized product comparisons, you can establish yourself as a trusted resource within your niche. Remember, transparency, balanced analysis, and a focus on providing valuable insights are crucial for building trust with your audience and ultimately driving successful affiliate sales. As you build your reputation as a reliable reviewer, your affiliate recommendations will hold greater weight, leading to a sustainable income stream for your e-commerce endeavours.

Building an Email List to Fuel Affiliate Marketing Success

BUILDING AN EMAIL LIST: Build an email list to nurture leads and promote affiliate products through targeted email campaigns. Segment your list based on interests to send highly relevant product recommendations that resonate with each subscriber segment.

Building an email list is an e-commerce marketer's secret weapon. It allows you to nurture leads, build relationships with potential customers, and ultimately drive targeted affiliate sales through personalized email campaigns. Here's a comprehensive guide to crafting an effective email list-building strategy and leveraging it to maximize your affiliate marketing efforts:

Crafting Compelling Lead Magnets:

◈ **Offer Valuable Content:** Provide free resources that genuinely solve problems or address specific needs within your niche. This could be an ebook, a cheat sheet, a discount code, or exclusive access to valuable content.

◈ **Targeted Lead Magnets:** Tailor your lead magnets to different audience segments. This increases their perceived value and encourages targeted list growth.

◈ **Landing Page Optimization:** Create high-converting landing pages that clearly explain the benefits of your lead magnet and capture email addresses seamlessly.

Growing Your Email List through Multiple Channels:

◈ **Website Opt-in Forms:** Strategically place opt-in forms throughout your website, such as sidebars, pop-ups (used strategically to avoid being intrusive), and after blog posts.

◈ **Social Media Integration:** Promote your lead magnet and opt-in forms across your social media platforms. Run targeted social media ads to reach a wider audience interested in your niche.

◈ **Content Marketing Integration:** Embed opt-in forms within your blog posts, YouTube video descriptions, or podcast episode show notes. Offer bonus content or exclusive insights accessible only through email subscription.

The Art of Email Nurturing and Segmentation:

◈ **Welcome Series:** Create a warm and informative welcome email series for new subscribers. This establishes your brand voice, sets expectations, and educates them about the value you offer.

◈ **Segmentation Strategies:** Segment your email list based on subscriber demographics, interests, purchase history, or engagement levels. This allows you to send highly relevant and personalized email campaigns that resonate with each segment.

◈ **Content Calendar and Cadence:** Develop an email content calendar and determine the optimal sending frequency. Aim for consistency without overwhelming subscribers.

Promoting Affiliate Products with Strategic Emails:

◈ **Product Recommendations:** Highlight affiliate products within your emails, focusing on solving specific customer pain points identified through segmentation.

◈ **Personalized Offers:** Tailor your product recommendations based on subscriber interests and purchase history. This significantly increases the relevance and potential impact of your emails.

◈ **Limited-Time Offers and Scarcity:** Create a sense of urgency by promoting exclusive discounts or limited-time offers for your affiliate products within your emails.

TRACKING PERFORMANCE and Optimizing Campaigns:

◈ **Email Marketing Tools:** Utilize email marketing tools to track key metrics such as open rates, click-through rates (CTRs), and conversion rates.

◈ **A/B Testing:** Test different subject lines, email formats, and call-to-action (CTA) buttons to see what resonates best with your audience. A/B testing helps you optimize your email campaigns for maximum impact.

◈ **Subscriber Feedback:** Encourage subscribers to provide feedback through surveys or polls embedded within your emails. Use their insights to refine your content strategy and deliver even greater value.

Building an engaged email list is a powerful asset for any affiliate marketer. By providing valuable content, segmenting your audience, and crafting targeted email promotions, you can nurture leads, promote affiliate products effectively, and ultimately drive sales and conversions. Remember, building trust and offering genuine value are key to fostering long-term relationships with your subscribers, transforming them into loyal customers who convert consistently through your affiliate links.

Leveraging Content Marketing to Sell Your Products and Services

◈ **Selling Your Own Products or Services:** Content creation can be a powerful tool to promote your own products (e.g., ebooks, online courses) or services (e.g., consulting, coaching). While promoting other companies' products can be lucrative, there's nothing quite like building your own brand and selling your unique offerings. Content creation can be a powerful tool in this endeavor, allowing you to establish yourself as an authority, nurture leads, and ultimately convert them into paying customers for your products (ebooks, online courses) or services (consulting, coaching). Here's a breakdown of how to leverage content marketing to propel your own brand and drive sales:

CONTENT STRATEGY TAILORED to Your Offerings:

◈ **Product-Centric Content:** Create valuable content directly related to your products or services. For eBooks, offer free sample chapters or cheat sheets. For online courses, share introductory lessons or behind-the-scenes glimpses. For consulting services, write articles showcasing your expertise in solving client challenges.

◈ **Targeted Audience:** Craft content that resonates with your ideal customer. Identify their pain points, aspirations, and preferred learning styles. Develop content that addresses their specific needs and positions you as the ultimate solution provider.

◇ **Content Diversification:** Don't limit yourself to one format. Explore a variety of content types, such as blog posts, info graphics, video tutorials, webinars, or even podcasts. This caters to different learning preferences and keeps your audience engaged.

Building Authority and Establishing Trust:

◇ **Demonstrate Expertise:** Share your knowledge and insights freely through your content. Position yourself as a thought leader within your niche by offering valuable information and actionable advice.

◇ **Case Studies and Testimonials:** Showcase the success stories of past clients or students who have benefited from your products or services. Social proof builds trust and credibility, encouraging potential customers to invest in your offerings.

◇ **Authentic Voice and Transparency:** Let your personality shine through your content. Be transparent about your approach and passionate about the value you deliver. This fosters genuine connections with your audience.

Nurturing Leads and Converting Customers:

◇ **Calls to Action (CTAs):** Strategically integrate clear CTAs within your content. Direct viewers/readers to sign up for your email list, download free resources related to your paid products, or schedule a consultation call to discuss your services.

◈ **Lead Magnets and Opt-in Forms:** Offer valuable lead magnets, like cheat sheets, templates, or exclusive content previews, in exchange for email addresses. This allows you to nurture leads and build relationships with potential customers.

◈ **Email Marketing Integration:** Develop targeted email campaigns that promote your products and services to your email list. Segment your audience based on interests and tailor your messaging accordingly.

Content Promotion and Building Reach:

◇ **Search Engine Optimization (SEO):** Optimize your content with relevant keywords to improve search engine ranking and organic traffic. Research keywords your target audience uses and ensure your content provides valuable information around those keywords.

◇ **Social Media Marketing:** Promote your content across your social media platforms to reach a wider audience. Engage with your followers, participate in relevant online communities, and run targeted social media ad campaigns.

◇ **Guest Blogging and Collaborations:** Partner with other influencers or bloggers in your niche. Contribute guest posts to their platforms or host joint webinars to expand your reach and tap into their audience base.

CONTENT ANALYTICS AND Continuous Improvement:

◇ **Track Performance Metrics:** Monitor key metrics like website traffic, email open rates, and conversion rates to understand how your content marketing efforts are performing.

◇ **Data-Driven Decisions:** Analyse data to identify what content resonates best with your audience. Focus on creating more content that generates high engagement and conversions.

◇ **Adapting to Trends and Audience Needs:** Stay updated on industry trends and audience preferences. Continuously adapt your content strategy to ensure it remains relevant and valuable to your target audience.

By crafting a strategic content marketing plan and consistently delivering valuable content, you can establish yourself as an authority, build trust with your audience, and ultimately convert them into loyal customers of your products and services. Remember, content marketing is a marathon, not a sprint. Focus on long-term value creation, audience engagement, and continuous optimization to build a thriving brand and achieve sustainable success.

Building a successful content creation strategy takes time and dedication. However, the rewards are substantial. By consistently creating valuable content, engaging with your audience, and leveraging the right monetization methods, you can turn your passion into a thriving online business.

Remember:

◈ **Quality over Quantity:** Focus on creating high-quality content that resonates with your audience.

◈ **Authenticity Matters:** Let your personality shine through and connect with your audience on a personal level.

◈ **Adapt and Evolve:** Be willing to adapt your content strategy based on audience feedback and industry trends.

◈ **Patience is Key:** Building a loyal audience takes time. Stay consistent and keep creating valuable content.

By following these steps and embracing the power of content creation, you can establish yourself as a thought leader, build a thriving online community, and achieve your entrepreneurial goals.

CRAFTING PROFITABLE Online Courses and Ebooks The internet has democratized knowledge sharing, making it easier than ever to transform your expertise into a revenue stream. If you possess valuable knowledge in a specific area, consider creating and selling online courses or ebooks. Here's a detailed exploration of these two content formats and how to leverage them to share your knowledge and generate income:

The Allure of Online Courses

- **Structured Learning Experiences:** Online courses offer a structured learning experience, allowing you to package your knowledge into digestible modules, videos, quizzes, and assignments. This caters to learners who prefer a progressive approach to knowledge acquisition.
- **Flexibility and Scalability:** Online courses offer unmatched flexibility for both you and your students. Students can learn at their own pace, revisit modules for review, and access the course content anytime, anywhere. This scalability allows you to reach a global audience without geographical limitations.
- **Platforms for Every Niche:** Numerous online course platforms cater to diverse niches and learning styles. Popular options include Udemy (broad range of topics), Skillshare (creative fields), Teachable (customizable platform), and Thinkific (all-in-one course creation suite).

Crafting Engaging and Profitable Online Courses:

- **Identify Your Niche and Target Audience:** Clearly define your area of expertise and identify your ideal student.

Understanding their needs, learning styles, and pain points is crucial for crafting a course that resonates with them.

-

- **Course Structure and Content Development:** Plan your course curriculum, outlining logical progression and addressing learning objectives within each module. Develop engaging content using a mix of video lectures, screencasts, downloadable resources, and interactive elements.

-

- **Pricing Strategy and Revenue Models:** Determine the pricing for your course based on its value proposition, production quality, and market competition. Consider offering subscription models, tiered course structures with bonus content, or lifetime access options.

The Power of Ebooks:

- **In-Depth Knowledge Sharing:** Ebooks allow you to delve deeper into a specific topic compared to online courses. They offer a convenient, portable format for learners to consume your knowledge at their leisure.

-

- **Lower Barrier to Entry:** Compared to online courses, ebooks often require less upfront investment in terms of production costs and technical setup. This makes them an accessible option for first-time knowledge entrepreneurs.

-

- **Global Distribution and Royalties:** Self-publishing platforms like Amazon Kindle Direct Publishing (KDP) allow for global distribution of your ebook. You earn royalties on every sale, creating a passive income stream that continues to generate revenue over time.

Creating High-Quality and Marketable Ebooks:

- **Topic Selection and Validation:** Choose a topic you're passionate about and with a proven market demand. Conduct keyword research to understand search trends and identify potential readers' interests.

- **Compelling Content and Engaging Writing Style:** Write clear, concise, and engaging content that educates and informs your readers. Structure your ebook logically, incorporate visuals like charts and graphs, and ensure it's professionally edited and formatted.

- **Marketing and Sales Strategies:** Promote your ebook through social media channels, email marketing, online communities, and targeted advertising. Consider offering free excerpts, participating in book promotions, and leveraging online review platforms.

BUILDING A SUSTAINABLE Knowledge Business:

- **Building an Audience and Community:** Focus on building an audience around your expertise, regardless of the format you choose. Engage with potential students or readers through blog posts, social media interaction, and guest appearances on relevant podcasts or webinars.

- **Value Creation and Consistent Delivery:** Focus on consistently delivering high-quality content, whether through online courses or ebooks. The value you provide determines your long-term success.

-

- **Adapting and Evolving:** Stay updated on industry trends and student/reader needs. Continuously refine your content, pricing strategies, and marketing approaches to maintain a competitive edge.

Beyond the Big Names: Exploring the Diverse Landscape of Online Course and E-book Platforms

WHILE UDEMY, SKILLSHARE, and Amazon Kindle Direct Publishing (KDP) are undeniably popular choices, the world of online learning and self-publishing offers a wealth of additional platforms to explore. Here's a breakdown of some key considerations when selecting the right platform for your online course or ebook, along with alternative options to consider:

Choosing the Right Platform:

◈ **Focus on Your Niche:** Different platforms cater to specific niches or learning styles. Udemy offers a broad range of topics, while Skillshare focuses more on creative fields. For highly specialized content, dedicated platforms might be a better fit.

◈ **Pricing and Revenue Models:** Compare platform fees, royalty structures, and available pricing models for courses or ebooks. Some platforms offer subscription models, while others focus on individual course sales.

◈ **Marketing and Community Features:** Consider the platform's marketing tools and built-in community features. Some platforms offer extensive marketing tools, while others prioritize student-instructor interaction through forums or discussion boards.

◈ **Technical Considerations:** Evaluate the platform's ease of use for course creation, upload functionalities, and student experience. Some platforms offer robust course creation suites, while others might require more technical expertise.

Alternative Platforms for Online Courses:

Teachable: Empowering Creators to Build Branded Online Empires

◇ **Teachable:** A user-friendly platform with extensive customization options and a focus on brand building for course creators. Teachable has carved a niche in the online course platform landscape by prioritizing user-friendliness, customization, and empowering creators to build their own brands. Let's delve deeper into what makes Teachable a compelling choice for aspiring online course creators:

USER-FRIENDLY COURSE Creation:

◇ **Drag-and-Drop Interface:** Teachable boasts a user-friendly interface that allows even beginners to create professional-looking courses. The drag-and-drop course builder simplifies uploading content like video lectures, PDFs, quizzes, and other learning materials.

◇ **Multiple Content Formats:** Teachable accommodates a variety of content formats for your courses. Integrate pre-recorded videos, live sessions, audio files, downloadable resources, and even text-based lessons to cater to diverse learning styles.

◇ **Drip Content and Scheduled Releases:** Maintain control over how students access your course content. Utilize drip content features to release modules or lessons on a predetermined schedule, keeping students engaged and coming back for more.

Building a Strong Brand Identity:

◈ **Customizable Branding:** Teachable allows you to personalize your course website with your own branding elements. This includes customizing the domain name, logo, color scheme, and overall look and feel to match your unique brand identity.

◈ **Landing Page Creation:** Develop custom landing pages specifically for your courses. Leverage Teachable's landing page builder to showcase your course offerings, highlight key benefits, and capture student email addresses for lead generation.

◈ **Marketing and Sales Tools:** Teachable equips you with essential marketing tools to promote your courses. Integrate email marketing tools, create coupon codes for promotions, and offer bundled course packages to incentivize sales.

Building a Community and Fostering Engagement:

◈ **Student Discussion Forums:** Teachable facilitates student interaction through built-in discussion forums. This allows students to ask questions, share insights, and connect with each other, fostering a sense of community within your course.

◈ **Direct Messaging:** Enable direct messaging functionality for students to communicate with you or other students privately. This personalized approach enhances the learning experience and allows you to provide targeted support.

◈ **Integrated Communities:** Connect your course with external communities like Facebook Groups or private forums. This expands student interaction opportunities and leverages existing online communities relevant to your course topic.

Additional Benefits of Teachable:

◇ **Multiple Pricing Options:** Teachable offers a range of pricing plans to suit your needs, from a free plan with limited features to higher tiers with increased course hosting capabilities, student enrolment limits, and custom domain options.

◇ **Sales Analytics and Reporting:** Track your course sales performance with detailed analytics and reporting tools. Monitor key metrics like student enrolment, completion rates, and revenue generated to gain valuable insights and optimize your course offerings.

◇ **Integrations with Third-Party Tools:** Teachable seamlessly integrates with various third-party tools. Connect your course with email marketing platforms, payment gateways, analytics tools, and marketing automation software to streamline your workflow.

Teachable is well-suited for course creators who value:

◇ **Brand Building:** Maintaining control over their brand identity and building a recognizable online presence.

◇ **Customization:** Personalizing the course experience for students and tailoring it to their specific learning needs.

◇ **Community Focus:** Fostering student interaction and fostering a sense of community within their courses.

If you're serious about building a branded online course empire, Teachable offers a compelling platform to turn your expertise into a thriving business. Remember, success hinges on consistently delivering valuable content, effectively marketing your courses, and nurturing relationships with your students. With the right strategy and Teachable's user-friendly tools, you can empower yourself to create and share your knowledge with the world, establishing yourself as a leader in your niche.

The All-Encompassing Course Creation Powerhouse

◈ **Thinkific:** An all-in-one course creation suite with built-in marketing tools, sales funnels, and membership features. Thinkific positions itself as a comprehensive solution for online course creators, offering an all-in-one suite that empowers you to create, market, sell, and deliver your courses seamlessly. Let's explore the features that make Thinkific a powerhouse for course creation and student engagement:

STREAMLINED COURSE Creation:

◈ **Intuitive Interface:** Thinkific boasts a user-friendly interface that simplifies the course creation process. Upload video lectures, PDFs, quizzes, and other learning materials with ease, even for beginners with no prior technical experience.

◈ **Multimedia Content Support:** Integrate a variety of content formats to cater to diverse learning styles. Thinkific supports video lectures, audio recordings, screencasts, downloadable resources, text-based modules, and even live sessions for a truly interactive learning experience.

◈ **Drip Content and Scheduled Releases:** Maintain control over how students access your course content. Utilize drip content features to release modules or lessons on a predetermined schedule, keeping students engaged and coming back for more.

Marketing and Sales Made Easy:

◇ **Built-in Marketing Tools:** Thinkific eliminates the need for multiple marketing platforms by offering integrated marketing tools within the platform itself. Create landing pages to showcase your courses, design sales funnels to convert website visitors into paying students, and leverage email marketing features to nurture leads and promote upcoming course launches.

◇ **Coupon Codes and Promotions:** Incentivize course enrollment with strategic promotions. Thinkific allows you to create coupon codes for discounts, limited-time offers, or bundled course packages to attract new students and boost sales.

◇ **Affiliate Marketing Integration:** Expand your reach and leverage the power of affiliate marketing. Thinkific allows you to recruit affiliates to promote your courses and earn commissions on each successful referral.

Membership Features and Community Building:

◇ **Membership Sites:** Thinkific goes beyond traditional course creation by offering membership site functionalities. Create subscription-based memberships that provide ongoing access to exclusive content, community forums, live events, or additional resources, fostering a loyal student base.

◇ **Discussion Forums and Communities:** Facilitate student interaction and build a strong learning community.

Thinkific's built-in discussion forums allow students to ask questions, share insights, and connect with each other, creating a more engaging learning environment.

◈ **Live Lessons and Webinars:** Host live lessons and webinars directly within Thinkific. This interactive format allows you to connect with students in real-time, answer questions, and provide more personalized learning experiences.

Additional Advantages of Thinkific:

◇ **Multiple Pricing Options:** Thinkific offers a range of pricing plans to suit your needs and budget. Start with a free plan to test the platform, or choose from higher tiers with increased course hosting capabilities, student enrolment limits, custom domain options, and advanced marketing features.

◇ **Detailed Sales Analytics:** Track your course performance and gain valuable insights with Thinkific's comprehensive analytics suite. Monitor key metrics like sales figures, student enrolment rates, completion rates, and student engagement levels to identify areas for improvement and optimize your course offerings.

◇ **Seamless Integrations:** Thinkific integrates seamlessly with a variety of third-party tools. Connect your courses with email marketing platforms, payment gateways, analytics tools, and marketing automation software to streamline your workflow and manage your online course business efficiently.

Thinkific is a powerful platform for course creators who value:

◇ **All-in-one Solution:** Consolidating course creation, marketing, sales, and community features under one roof, simplifying course management.

◇ **Marketing and Sales Automation:** Leveraging built-in marketing tools and sales funnels to convert website visitors into paying students.

◇ **Membership Site Functionality:** Offering recurring revenue streams through membership subscriptions and providing ongoing value to students.

If you're looking for a comprehensive platform that empowers you to create high-quality courses, market them effectively, and build a thriving online learning community, Thinkific is a strong contender. Remember, success in the online course landscape requires a commitment to creating valuable content, consistently delivering a positive learning experience, and actively engaging with your students. With Thinkific's robust set of features, you can streamline your course creation workflow, focus on what you do best – sharing your knowledge – and establish yourself as a trusted authority in your chosen niche.

Cultivating Engaged Communities through Courses and Memberships

◇ **Podia:** A platform designed for selling memberships alongside online courses, ideal for creators offering ongoing content and community access. Podia stands out in the online course platform landscape by offering a unique blend of course creation and membership site functionalities. This makes it ideal for creators who want to nurture a loyal community around their expertise, providing ongoing content and exclusive access in exchange for recurring revenue. Here's a closer look at what makes Podia a compelling choice for fostering engaged communities through online courses and memberships:

SEAMLESS COURSE CREATION and Management:

◇ **User-Friendly Interface:** Podia offers a user-friendly interface that simplifies course creation, even for beginners. Upload video lectures, PDFs, quizzes, and other learning materials with ease, ensuring a smooth content delivery experience for your students.

◇ **Multiple Content Formats:** Cater to diverse learning styles by integrating a variety of content formats within your courses. Podia supports video lectures, audio recordings, screencasts, downloadable resources, text-based modules, and even drip content features to control the release schedule and keep students engaged.

◈ **Bundled Offerings:** Create bundled course packages that combine multiple courses at a discounted price. This incentivizes students to invest in a broader range of your educational offerings and provides them with a more comprehensive learning experience.

Thriving Membership Communities:

◈ **Membership Site Functionality:** Podia allows you to create membership sites alongside your online courses. This opens doors for recurring revenue streams by offering exclusive content, ongoing access to resources, private community forums, live events, or Q&A sessions for members.

◈ **Membership Levels and Tiers:** Cater to different budgets and needs by offering tiered membership options. This allows you to provide varying levels of access and benefits based on membership level, encouraging higher subscription tiers for a premium learning experience.

◈ **Community Building Features:** Facilitate interaction and build a strong community within your membership site. Podia offers built-in discussion forums, comments sections, and messaging features, allowing members to connect, share insights, and support each other's learning journeys.

Additional Advantages of Podia:

◈ **All-in-One Platform:** Podia streamlines your workflow by consolidating course creation, membership management, email marketing, and sales functionalities under one roof.

This simplifies course and community management, saving you time and effort.

◈ **Monetization Options:** Podia empowers you to choose from various monetization options. Sell courses as one-time purchases, offer free trials for courses or memberships, leverage recurring subscriptions for memberships, or even combine these strategies to create a flexible revenue model.

◈ **Beautiful Storefronts:** Podia automatically generates beautiful landing pages for your online courses and memberships. This allows you to showcase your offerings in a professional and visually appealing manner, fostering trust and encouraging potential students and members to enrol.

◈ **Podia is well-suited for creators who:**

◈ **Value Community Building:** Prioritize fostering a loyal student base through ongoing content, exclusive access, and interactive community features within their membership sites.

◈ **Offer Ongoing Value:** Develop course curriculums with the intention of providing continual learning experiences and resources for students who invest in memberships.

◈ **Seek Flexibility:** Desire a platform that allows them to combine one-time course sales with recurring revenue streams generated through memberships.

If you're passionate about sharing your knowledge and fostering a thriving online community, Podia equips you with the tools to build a sustainable business model. Remember, consistent content creation, engaging with your community members, and adapting your offerings based on member needs are crucial for success. With Podia's all-in-one platform and focus on memberships, you can cultivate a dedicated following, establish yourself as a trusted authority, and generate ongoing income by sharing your expertise with the world.

A comprehensive membership platform.

◈ **Kajabi, with course hosting**, marketing tools, and email marketing features all under one roof. If you're looking to build a multifaceted online business that goes beyond just selling courses, Kajabi empowers you to create a one-stop shop for your audience. By providing valuable learning experiences, fostering a loyal community through memberships, and leveraging Kajabi's comprehensive suite of tools, you can establish yourself as a leader in your niche and generate sustainable income by sharing your expertise with the world. Remember, success hinges on consistently delivering high-quality content, actively engaging with your audience, and adapting your offerings based on their needs and market trends. With Kajabi as your platform, you can turn your passions and knowledge into a thriving online business.

Alternative Platforms for E-books:

Smashwords: Broadening Your E-book's Reach beyond Amazon

SMASHWORDS: This platform distributes ebooks to a wide range of online retailers like Apple iBook's, Barnes & Noble Nook, and Kobo, offering broader reach beyond Amazon.

While Amazon's Kindle Direct Publishing (KDP) is a juggernaut in the ebook market, it's not the only game in town. Smashwords offers a compelling alternative for self-published authors seeking to maximize their ebook's reach and visibility. Here's a breakdown of what makes Smashwords a valuable tool for expanding your ebook's distribution beyond Amazon:

Wider Retail Network

Multiple Retailer Distribution: Smashwords acts as an aggregator, distributing your ebook to a vast network of online retailers across the globe. This includes major players like Apple iBook's, Barnes & Noble Nook, Kobo, Google Play, and Rakuten Kobo, significantly increasing your e-book's potential audience compared to relying solely on Amazon.

Library Distribution: Gain access to library markets through Smashwords' partnerships with library lending platforms. This exposes your ebook to a new audience of library patrons who borrow ebooks instead of purchasing them, potentially leading to increased brand awareness and future sales.

Global Reach and Multiple Formats:

International Distribution: Smashwords facilitates international distribution, making your ebook available to readers worldwide. This opens doors to new markets and allows you to tap into a broader audience base beyond your local region.

Multiple Ebook Formats: Smashwords ensures your ebook is available in various industry-standard formats, including EPUB, MOBI (compatible with Kindles), and others. This caters to readers who use different e-reading devices and software, eliminating format compatibility barriers.

Additional Benefits of Smashwords:

Free Distribution: Unlike some aggregators, Smashwords offers free ebook distribution services. You only pay a small fee per sale, making it a cost-effective option for self-published authors, especially those just starting out.

Marketing and Sales Tools: Smashwords provides basic marketing and sales tools to help you promote your ebook. Leverage features like pre-order options, coupon codes for promotions, and the ability to embed sample chapters to generate interest and drive sales.

Detailed Sales Reporting: Track your ebook's performance across different retailers with detailed sales reports. Gain insights into reader behaviour, identify your strongest sales channels, and make informed decisions about future marketing strategies.

Things to Consider with Smashwords:

◇ **Limited Control:** Compared to KDP, Smashwords offers less control over pricing and discounting for your ebook on different retail platforms.

◇ **Marketing Effort Required:** Smashwords primarily focuses on distribution. The onus of marketing your ebook and generating reader interest lies primarily with the author.

WHO SHOULD CONSIDER Smashwords?

◇ **Self-Published Authors Seeking Wider Reach:** If you want your ebook to be available on a wider range of platforms and reach a broader audience beyond Amazon, Smashwords is an excellent option.

◇ **Authors Targeting International Markets:** Smashwords' global distribution capabilities make it ideal for authors who want to reach readers worldwide.

◇ **Cost-Conscious Authors:** Smashwords' free distribution model makes it an attractive choice for self-published authors on a budget.

By leveraging Smashwords alongside KDP or as an alternative distribution channel, you can significantly increase your e-book's visibility and sales potential. Remember, success in the self-publishing world hinges on a combination of factors: a high-quality ebook, effective marketing strategies, and reaching your target audience on the platforms they frequent. Smashwords empowers you to expand your reach, connect with a wider audience, and take your self-published book to the next level.

Expanding Your Ebook's Reach with Flexibility and Control

DRAFT2DIGITAL: Similar to Smashwords, this platform distributes ebooks to multiple retailers and libraries, maximizing exposure potential. Draft2Digital (D2D) carves its niche in the ebook distribution landscape by offering a robust and user-friendly platform for self-published authors. Similar to Smashwords, D2D prioritizes maximizing your ebook's exposure by distributing it to a vast network of retailers and libraries. However, D2D goes a step further by providing authors with greater control over pricing, discounting, and marketing strategies. Here's a detailed look at what makes Draft2Digital a compelling choice for self-published authors seeking wider reach and control over their ebooks:

Extensive Distribution Network:

Multiple Retailer Coverage: D2D distributes your ebook to a comprehensive network of online retailers, including major players like Apple iBooks, Barnes & Noble Nook, Kobo, Google Play, and Rakuten Kobo. This broadens your audience reach significantly compared to relying solely on Amazon.

Library Marketing and Distribution: D2D partners with library lending platforms, making your ebook accessible to library patrons who borrow ebooks. This exposes your work to a new audience and fosters brand awareness, potentially leading to future sales.

Enhanced Control and Flexibility:

Pricing and Discounting Freedom: D2D empowers you to set your own ebook price and offer targeted discounts across different retail channels. This allows you to tailor your pricing strategy to maximize sales and reach new audiences through strategic promotions.

Pre-Order Options and Marketing Tools: Generate pre-order buzz and excitement for your ebook launch. D2D offers pre-order functionality and basic marketing tools such as coupon codes and sample chapter embedding to pique reader interest and drive sales.

Detailed Sales Reporting and Analytics: Track your ebook's performance comprehensively across various retail platforms. D2D's detailed sales reporting offers valuable insights into reader behavior, allowing you to identify strong sales channels, optimize pricing strategies, and refine your marketing efforts.

Additional Advantages of Draft2Digital:

COST-EFFECTIVE DISTRIBUTION: D2D utilizes a pay-per-sale model, charging a small fee only when your ebook sells. This cost-effective approach minimizes upfront investment and maximizes potential profit margins, particularly for authors with multiple ebook titles.

Multiple Format Conversion: Draft2Digital seamlessly converts your ebook manuscript into various industry-standard formats, including EPUB, MOBI, and others. This ensures compatibility with different e-reading devices and software, eliminating format barriers for your readers.

User-Friendly Platform: D2D boasts an intuitive interface that simplifies the ebook upload, distribution, and reporting process. Even tech-averse authors can navigate the platform with ease and manage their ebooks effectively.

Who Should Consider Draft2Digital?

Authors Seeking Wide Distribution and Control: D2D offers a balance between extensive distribution like Smashwords and the pricing and marketing control of KDP. This makes it ideal for authors who want to reach a broad audience while maintaining control over their ebook's pricing and promotion.

Cost-Conscious Authors with Multiple Ebooks: The pay-per-sale model makes D2D an attractive option for authors with multiple ebooks, as upfront costs are minimized.

Tech-Savvy Authors Who Value User-Friendliness: D2D's intuitive interface is perfect for authors who appreciate a user-friendly platform for managing their ebook distribution.

By leveraging Draft2Digital's extensive distribution network, control over pricing and marketing, and user-friendly platform, you can effectively broaden your eBook's reach, connect with a wider audience, and maximize your self-publishing success. Remember, a high-quality ebook, strategic marketing efforts, and reaching readers on the platforms they frequent are crucial for success. D2D empowers you to navigate these aspects effectively and establish yourself as a prominent voice in the self-publishing landscape.

Apple iBooks Author
Crafting Ebooks Tailored for the Apple Ecosystem

APPLE IBOOK'S AUTHOR: This software allows you to create and publish ebooks specifically for the Apple iBook's store, ideal if you have a strong Apple user base.

While platforms like Draft2Digital and Smashwords offer widespread ebook distribution, Apple iBooks Author caters to a specific niche. This software empowers you to create and publish ebooks specifically for the Apple iBooks store, making it ideal for authors who want to tap into the vast Apple user base and leverage unique multimedia features. Here's a closer look at what makes Apple iBooks Author a valuable tool for crafting engaging ebooks for Apple users:

Rich Multimedia Integration:

Interactive Elements: Apple iBooks Author goes beyond traditional text and images. Integrate interactive elements like quizzes, 3D objects, animations, and even audio or video files within your ebook. This creates a more dynamic and engaging reading experience for Apple device users.

Seamless Apple Ecosystem Integration: Leverage the power of the Apple ecosystem. Link seamlessly to other Apple apps like Maps, Music, or even iBooks references within your ebook, providing a richer and more interconnected reading experience for Apple users.

Stunning Visual Design: Apple iBooks Author offers a user-friendly interface with drag-and-drop functionality. Design visually appealing ebooks with customizable layouts, elegant typography options, and high-quality image integration, creating a professional and polished look.

Reaching the Apple User Base:

Targeted Distribution: Publish your ebook directly to the Apple iBooks store, giving you access to millions of potential readers who use iPhones, iPads, and Macs. This allows you to focus on a specific demographic – Apple device users – and cater your content accordingly.

Brand Consistency: Maintain a consistent brand identity across your Apple ecosystem. Apple iBooks Author allows you to integrate your existing branding elements, including logos, fonts, and color schemes, ensuring your ebook aligns seamlessly with your overall brand image.

Things to Consider with Apple iBooks Author:

Limited Distribution: Apple iBooks Author restricts distribution solely to the Apple iBooks store. This limits your ebook's reach compared to platforms like D2Digital or Smashwords, which distribute to a wider range of retailers.

Technical Requirements: Apple iBooks Author is a Mac-only software. If you don't use a Mac computer, you'll need access to one to create and publish your ebook using this platform.

Who Should Consider Apple iBooks Author?

Authors Targeting Apple Users: If you have a strong existing audience within the Apple user base or your content caters specifically to Apple devices, iBooks Author is a compelling platform to reach your target readers directly.

Authors Who Value Multimedia Features: If you envision your ebook as a richly interactive experience with multimedia elements and Apple ecosystem integration, iBooks Author provides the tools to bring your vision to life.

Mac Users with Existing Apple Branding: For Mac users who already have established brand elements for their creative work, iBooks Author simplifies the ebook creation process and ensures seamless brand consistency.

By leveraging the unique features of Apple iBooks Author, you can create engaging and visually stunning ebooks tailored for the Apple user base. Remember, while iBooks Author offers a targeted approach, consider using it alongside wider distribution platforms like D2Digital or Smashwords to maximize your ebook's potential reach. With a high-quality ebook, strategic marketing efforts, and reaching readers on their preferred platforms, you can achieve success in the self-publishing world.

A One-Stop Shop for Self-Publishing Ebooks and Print-on-Demand Books

◈ **Lulu:** This platform offers self-publishing for both ebooks and print-on-demand books, catering to creators who might want to explore physical book sales alongside digital formats. Lulu stands out in the self-publishing landscape by offering a comprehensive solution for creators who want to explore both digital and physical book formats. Whether you envision your work as an ebook, a paperback, a hardcover, or even a combination, Lulu empowers you to bring your vision to life with a user-friendly platform and a global print-on-demand network. Here's a breakdown of what makes Lulu a compelling choice for self-publishers seeking to bridge the gap between ebooks and physical books:

SEAMLESS EBOOK AND Print-on-Demand (POD) Integration:

Unified Platform: Lulu streamlines the self-publishing process by offering ebook and POD book publishing under one roof. Upload your manuscript, design your cover, set your pricing, and publish your work in both digital and physical formats with ease.

Format Conversion: Lulu simplifies ebook formatting for various platforms like Apple iBooks, Kobo, and Barnes & Noble Nook. Focus on creating your content, and Lulu takes care of ensuring your ebook is compatible with different reading devices and software.

Global Print-on-Demand Network: Tap into Lulu's extensive print-on-demand network. Your books are printed only when they are ordered, eliminating the need for upfront inventory investment and minimizing storage requirements.

Customization and Control:

Design Tools and Templates: Lulu offers a range of design tools and templates to help you create professional looking book covers and layouts, even for beginners with no prior graphic design experience.

Pricing and Distribution Control: Set your own prices for both ebooks and printed books. Choose which retailers you want your ebook to be distributed to and leverage Lulu's global network to reach a wider audience.

Marketing and Sales Tools: Lulu provides basic marketing and sales tools to help you promote your books. Integrate social media sharing buttons, offer coupon codes for promotions, and leverage Lulu's online bookstore to showcase your work.

Additional Advantages of Lulu:

Free Basic Plan: Lulu offers a free plan that allows you to publish one book (either ebook or print) with basic features. This is a great option for first-time self-publishers to test the platform and get comfortable with the process.

Detailed Sales Reporting and Analytics

Track your book sales performance for both ebooks and printed books. Gain insights into reader behaviour, identify your strongest sales channels, and make informed decisions about future marketing strategies.

Community and Support: Lulu offers a supportive community forum where you can connect with other self-published authors, share experiences, and learn from each other's successes and challenges.

Who Should Consider Lulu?

Authors Who Want Both Ebook and Print Options: If you envision your work being available in both digital and physical formats, Lulu provides a convenient and cost-effective solution.

Cost-Conscious Self-Publishers: Lulu's free basic plan and print-on-demand model minimize upfront costs, making it an attractive option for authors on a budget.

First-Time Self-Publishers: Lulu's user-friendly platform and basic features are well-suited for beginners who are new to the self-publishing world.

By leveraging Lulu's all-in-one platform for ebooks and POD books, you gain the flexibility to cater to diverse reader preferences. Some readers might prefer the convenience of an ebook, while others might value the tangible experience of holding a physical book in their hands. Lulu empowers you to reach both audiences seamlessly, maximize your book's sales potential, and establish yourself as a successful self-published author. Remember, success hinges on creating high-quality content, effectively marketing your books, and understanding your target audience's preferences. With Lulu's tools and resources, you can navigate both the digital and physical book landscapes and share your work with the world.

Additional Considerations:

A Path to Complete Control (But More Work)

BUILDING YOUR OWN WEBSITE: Consider building a standalone website to host your courses or ebooks. This offers maximum control over branding, pricing, and customer relationships, but requires more technical expertise and marketing effort. Choosing to host your courses or ebooks on a standalone website offers the ultimate level of control over your brand, pricing, and customer interactions. While this approach grants significant advantages, it also necessitates a greater investment in technical expertise and marketing efforts. Let's delve deeper into the pros and cons of building your own website:

Unmatched Control and Flexibility:

Brand Identity: Craft a website that flawlessly reflects your unique brand image. From design elements to content voice, you have complete control over how you present yourself and your offerings to potential customers.

Pricing Freedom: Set your own prices for courses or ebooks, and design custom pricing structures like tiered memberships or bundle deals. You're not limited by the pricing models of pre-built platforms.

Direct Customer Relationships: Build a direct relationship with your audience by collecting customer data and managing all communication channels through your website. This fosters stronger customer loyalty and allows for personalized marketing strategies.

Customization and Integrations: Tailor your website's functionality and features to your specific needs. Integrate with various tools for email marketing, payment processing, membership management, or community forums, creating a seamless user experience.

Challenges and Considerations:

Technical Expertise: Building and maintaining a website requires some degree of technical knowledge. You'll need to understand website hosting, domain registration, content management systems (CMS), and potentially security measures. If you lack this expertise, consider hiring a web developer or using a user-friendly website builder platform with limitations.

Marketing and Promotion: Driving traffic to your website is crucial for attracting potential customers. Be prepared to invest time and resources in marketing your courses or ebooks through various channels, like social media marketing, search engine optimization (SEO), or paid advertising.

Ongoing Maintenance: Websites require ongoing maintenance to ensure security, functionality, and optimal performance. This includes updating plugins, managing backups, and addressing any technical issues that may arise.

Who Should Consider Building Their Own Website?

ESTABLISHED CREATORS with a Loyal Audience: If you already have a strong brand presence and a dedicated following, building your own website allows you to leverage your existing audience and maximize control over the customer experience.

Tech-Savvy Individuals or Teams: If you or someone on your team possesses the technical expertise required for website development and maintenance, building your own platform offers a high degree of customization and control.

Creators Offering Unique or Complex Courses: If your courses or ebooks require specific features or integrations not readily available on pre-built platforms, building your own website allows for tailored functionality to meet your unique needs. While building your own website offers undeniable advantages in terms of control and flexibility, it's not a decision to take lightly. Carefully evaluate your technical expertise, marketing capabilities, and the specific needs of your courses or ebooks before embarking on this path.

Here are some additional factors to consider

Scalability: Can your website infrastructure handle a growing audience and potential surges in traffic?

Payment Processing: Choose a secure and reliable payment gateway to ensure a smooth transaction experience for your customers.

Customer Support: How will you handle customer inquiries and provide support to your audience?

By carefully considering these factors, you can determine if building your own website is the right move for your online learning or ebook business. Remember, success hinges on creating valuable content, effectively marketing your offerings, and providing a positive customer experience. If you're willing to invest the time and effort, building your own website can be a powerful tool to establish yourself as a leader in your niche and achieve long-term success.

Taking Control of Your Revenue Stream (But With More Responsibility)

◈ **Direct Sales and Subscriptions:** Explore the option of selling your courses or ebooks directly from your website through secure payment gateways and subscription management tools. This eliminates platform fees but necessitates managing customer acquisition and support independently. Selling your courses or ebooks directly from your website offers an enticing path to maximize your profits. By eliminating platform fees associated with third-party marketplaces, you retain a larger share of your revenue. However, this approach comes with the responsibility of managing customer acquisition, payment processing, and ongoing customer support. Let's delve deeper into the advantages and considerations of direct sales and subscriptions on your own website:

FINANCIAL ADVANTAGES and Control:

◈ **Higher Profit Margins:** Eliminate platform fees and keep a larger portion of your revenue from each sale. This can significantly boost your profitability, especially with high-volume sales or premium-priced courses/ebooks.

◈ **Flexible Pricing and Promotions:** Design custom pricing structures that best suit your offerings. Implement tiered subscriptions for course bundles, offer discount codes for promotions, or experiment with different pricing models to optimize your revenue generation.

◇ **Upselling and Cross-Selling Opportunities:** Leverage your website to directly promote related courses, ebooks, or merchandise to existing customers. This increases the average value of each customer transaction and opens doors for recurring revenue streams.

Building Direct Customer Relationships:

◇ **Own Your Customer Data:** Collect customer data directly through your website, allowing you to build targeted email marketing campaigns, personalize customer experiences, and foster stronger brand loyalty.

◇ **Direct Communication and Feedback:** Facilitate direct communication channels with your customers. Address inquiries, gather feedback, and build a community around your offerings, fostering a more engaged audience.

◇ **Control over Branding and User Experience:** Craft a website that flawlessly reflects your brand identity and provides a seamless user experience for your customers. You control the design, layout, and overall customer journey on your platform.

Challenges and Considerations:

◇ **Customer Acquisition and Marketing:** The onus of attracting potential customers falls entirely on you. Invest in marketing strategies like search engine optimization (SEO), social media marketing, or paid advertising to drive traffic to your website.

◇ **Payment Processing and Security:** Implement secure payment gateways to ensure a smooth and safe transaction experience for your customers. Be mindful of PCI compliance and data security regulations.

◇ **Customer Support and Management:** Provide prompt and efficient customer support to address inquiries, troubleshoot issues, and handle refunds. Building a robust customer support system is crucial for maintaining customer satisfaction.

◇ **Technical Expertise:** Managing a website requires some technical knowledge, especially for aspects like security updates, maintenance, and potential integrations with payment gateways or email marketing tools.

Who Should Consider Direct Sales and Subscriptions?

◇ **Established Creators with a Loyal Audience:** If you already have a dedicated following and a strong brand presence, selling directly from your website allows you to leverage your existing audience base and maximize profit margins.

◇ **Content Creators with Unique Offerings:** If your courses or ebooks cater to a specific niche or require unique features not readily available on pre-built platforms, selling directly allows you to offer a tailored user experience.

◇ **Tech-Savvy Individuals or Teams:** If you or someone on your team possesses the technical expertise to manage website development, payment processing, and customer support, direct sales offer a high degree of control and customization.

Additional Considerations:

◈ **Subscription Management Tools:** Explore subscription management tools to automate recurring billing, manage member access to content, and streamline the subscription experience for both you and your customers.

◈ **Email Marketing Integration:** Integrate email marketing tools with your website to nurture leads, promote your offerings, and stay engaged with your audience.

◈ **Content Security:** Implement measures to protect your copyrighted content from unauthorized access or distribution, especially for courses with downloadable materials.

Direct sales and subscriptions

Direct sales and subscriptions empower you to take control of your revenue stream and build a direct relationship with your audience. However, be prepared to invest time and resources in marketing, customer support, and website management. By carefully weighing the advantages and challenges, you can determine if this approach aligns with your goals and capabilities. Remember, success hinges on creating valuable content, providing exceptional customer service, and continuously refining your marketing strategies to reach your target audience effectively. With dedication and a well-crafted plan, direct sales and subscriptions can be a powerful path to long-term success in the online course or ebook market.

Choosing the right platform

Choosing the right platform is a crucial step in your online course or ebook venture. By carefully evaluating your needs, target audience, and technical capabilities, you can select a platform that empowers you to effectively share your knowledge and build a thriving knowledge business. Remember, the online learning and self-publishing landscape is constantly evolving, so stay informed about emerging platforms and adapt your approach accordingly.

By leveraging the power of online courses and ebooks, you can share your expertise with the world, establish yourself as a thought leader, and generate a sustainable income stream. Remember, focus on providing exceptional value, building a loyal audience, and continuously refining your offerings to thrive in the ever-evolving knowledge-sharing landscape.

Direct Sales and Subscriptions

Taking Control of Your Revenue Stream (But With More Responsibility)

DIRECT SALES AND SUBSCRIPTIONS: Explore the option of selling your courses or ebooks directly from your website through secure payment gateways and subscription management tools. This eliminates platform fees but necessitates managing customer acquisition and support independently. Selling your courses or ebooks directly from your website offers an enticing path to maximize your profits. By eliminating platform fees associated with third-party marketplaces, you retain a larger share of your revenue. However, this approach comes with the responsibility of managing customer acquisition, payment processing, and ongoing customer support. Let's delve deeper into the advantages and considerations of direct sales and subscriptions on your own website:

Financial Advantages and Control:

Higher Profit Margins: Eliminate platform fees and keep a larger portion of your revenue from each sale. This can significantly boost your profitability, especially with high-volume sales or premium-priced courses/ebooks.

Flexible Pricing and Promotions: Design custom pricing structures that best suit your offerings. Implement tiered subscriptions for course bundles, offer discount codes for promotions, or experiment with different pricing models to optimize your revenue generation.

Upselling and Cross-Selling Opportunities: Leverage your website to directly promote related courses, ebooks, or merchandise to existing customers. This increases the average value of each customer transaction and opens doors for recurring revenue streams.

Building Direct Customer Relationships:

Own Your Customer Data: Collect customer data directly through your website, allowing you to build targeted email marketing campaigns, personalize customer experiences, and foster stronger brand loyalty.

Direct Communication and Feedback: Facilitate direct communication channels with your customers. Address inquiries, gather feedback, and build a community around your offerings, fostering a more engaged audience.

Control over Branding and User Experience: Craft a website that flawlessly reflects your brand identity and provides a seamless user experience for your customers. You control the design, layout, and overall customer journey on your platform.

Challenges and Considerations:

Customer Acquisition and Marketing: The onus of attracting potential customers falls entirely on you. Invest in marketing strategies like search engine optimization (SEO), social media marketing, or paid advertising to drive traffic to your website.

Payment Processing and Security: Implement secure payment gateways to ensure a smooth and safe transaction experience for your customers. Be mindful of PCI compliance and data security regulations.

Customer Support and Management: Provide prompt and efficient customer support to address inquiries, troubleshoot issues, and handle refunds. Building a robust customer support system is crucial for maintaining customer satisfaction.

Technical Expertise: Managing a website requires some technical knowledge, especially for aspects like security updates, maintenance, and potential integrations with payment gateways or email marketing tools.

Who Should Consider Direct Sales and Subscriptions?

ESTABLISHED CREATORS with a Loyal Audience: If you already have a dedicated following and a strong brand presence, selling directly from your website allows you to leverage your existing audience base and maximize profit margins.

Content Creators with Unique Offerings: If your courses or ebooks cater to a specific niche or require unique features not readily available on pre-built platforms, selling directly allows you to offer a tailored user experience.

Tech-Savvy Individuals or Teams: If you or someone on your team possesses the technical expertise to manage website development, payment processing, and customer support, direct sales offer a high degree of control and customization.

Additional Considerations:

Subscription Management Tools: Explore subscription management tools to automate recurring billing, manage member access to content, and streamline the subscription experience for both you and your customers.

Email Marketing Integration: Integrate email marketing tools with your website to nurture leads, promote your offerings, and stay engaged with your audience.

Content Security: Implement measures to protect your copyrighted content from unauthorized access or distribution, especially for courses with downloadable materials.

Direct sales and subscriptions empower you to take control of your revenue stream and build a direct relationship with your audience. However, be prepared to invest time and resources in marketing, customer support, and website management. By carefully weighing the advantages and challenges, you can determine if this approach aligns with your goals and capabilities. Remember, success hinges on creating valuable content, providing exceptional customer service, and continuously refining your marketing strategies to reach your target audience effectively. With dedication and a well-crafted plan, direct sales and subscriptions can be a powerful path to long-term success in the online course or ebook market. Choosing the right platform is a crucial step in your online course or ebook venture. By carefully evaluating your needs, target audience, and technical capabilities, you can select a platform that empowers you to effectively share your knowledge and build a thriving knowledge business. Remember, the online learning and self-publishing landscape is constantly evolving, so stay informed about emerging platforms and adapt your approach accordingly.

By leveraging the power of online courses and ebooks, you can share your expertise with the world, establish yourself as a thought leader, and generate a sustainable income stream. Remember, focus on providing exceptional value, building a loyal audience, and continuously refining your offerings to thrive in the ever-evolving knowledge-sharing landscape.

Exploring the Diverse Landscape of Online Income Generation

WHILE CREATING AND selling courses or ebooks offers a compelling path to online income, it's not the only option. The digital world presents a vast array of opportunities to generate revenue, each with its own advantages, requirements, and earning potential. Here's a glimpse into some alternative methods of making money online, categorized by their income potential:

Lower Earning Potential Options:

Unveiling the Reality of Online Surveys: Convenience with Limited Earning Potential

ONLINE SURVEYS: Websites and apps offer rewards for completing surveys and sharing your opinions. While convenient and accessible, surveys typically pay very little per completion, making it difficult to generate substantial income. Online surveys offer a seemingly effortless way to make money online. Websites and apps abound, promising rewards for completing questionnaires and sharing your opinions on various topics. While the attraction of earning from the comfort of your couch is undeniable, it's crucial to understand the limitations of online surveys before diving in. Here's a deeper look at the world of online surveys, exploring their advantages and disadvantages to help you decide if they fit your income generation goals:

Advantages of Online Surveys:

Flexibility and Accessibility: Participate in surveys anytime, anywhere with an internet connection. No commute or specific work hours are required, making them ideal for stay-at-home parents, students, or individuals with flexible schedules.

Low Barrier to Entry: No special skills or qualifications are needed. Most surveys are open to anyone who meets the age and demographic requirements.

Easy to Start: Signing up for survey websites and apps is quick and straightforward. Complete a profile to ensure you receive surveys relevant to your demographics, and you're ready to begin.

Passive Income Potential: Surveys can be completed while multitasking, like watching TV or listening to music. While the earnings may be low per survey, they can contribute to a small stream of passive income if done consistently.

Disadvantages of Online Surveys:

Low Earnings per Survey: Rewards for completing surveys are typically meagre, often ranging from a few cents to a dollar or two. Generating a substantial income solely through surveys requires a significant time investment and participation in a high volume of surveys.

Disqualification: Surveys often screen participants based on demographics or specific answer choices. You may invest time in starting a survey only to be disqualified later, receiving no compensation.

Limited Earning Potential: There's a cap on how much you can realistically earn through surveys. The time commitment required to generate a meaningful income often outweighs the potential rewards.

Repetitive and Time-Consuming: Surveys can be monotonous and repetitive, especially if you participate in a large volume. The time spent completing surveys might be better utilized in pursuing other income generation opportunities.

Alternatives to Consider:

Microtasking Platforms: Similar to surveys, microtasking platforms offer small rewards for completing simple online tasks like data entry, image tagging, or short writing assignments. While the earnings per task are low, they can be slightly higher than surveys and offer a similar level of flexibility.

Freelancing Platforms: If you possess specific skills like writing, editing, graphic design, or programming, consider freelancing platforms. Offer your services to clients and set your own rates. This requires more upfront effort to establish your profile and secure projects, but the earning potential is significantly higher compared to surveys.

Online Tutoring: Share your knowledge and expertise by tutoring students online. Platforms connect tutors with students in various subjects. Earnings depend on your qualifications and experience, but offer a higher earning potential than surveys with a more direct impact on others.

Who Might Benefit from Online Surveys?

Individuals Seeking Supplemental Income: If you're looking for a way to earn a few extra dollars here and there, and have time to spare, online surveys can be a convenient option. However, don't expect to replace your full-time income with surveys alone.

Stay-at-Home Parents or Students with Flexible Schedules: The flexibility of online surveys can be attractive for those with time constraints. Complete surveys during nap times or between classes to generate a small additional income stream.

The Bottom Line:

Online surveys offer a low-barrier entry point to online income generation. However, their limited earning potential makes them unsuitable for those seeking a significant income source. Carefully consider the time commitment required versus the potential rewards before dedicating a significant amount of time to online surveys. Explore alternative options that might provide a better return on your time and effort in the long run.

Unveiling the World of Website and App Testing

TESTING WEBSITES AND Apps: Companies seek user feedback to improve their websites and apps. Testing involves navigating interfaces, completing tasks, and reporting bugs or suggesting improvements. Earnings per test vary, but it's generally considered a low-earning activity.The digital landscape thrives on user experience. Companies constantly strive to improve their websites and apps, and that's where website and app testers come in. These testers act as digital guinea pigs, navigating interfaces, completing tasks, and providing valuable feedback to help developers identify and address usability issues. While contributing to the creation of polished digital products is rewarding, it's important to understand the realities of website and app testing, particularly regarding earning potential. Let's delve deeper into this field, exploring its advantages, disadvantages, and who might find it a suitable fit.

Advantages of Website and App Testing:

◈ **Flexible Work Schedule:** Testing opportunities are often available on flexible schedules. Fit testing sessions around your existing commitments, making it a good option for students, stay-at-home parents, or those seeking a side hustle.

◈ **No Prior Experience Required:** Unlike some online income avenues, website and app testing generally doesn't require specific technical skills. The ability to follow instructions, provide clear feedback, and navigate user interfaces effectively are the key qualities companies seek.

◇ **Remote Work Opportunity:** Testing can be done from the comfort of your own home, eliminating the need for commutes or adhering to a specific work environment.

◇ **Contribute to Product Development:** Play a role in shaping the user experience of digital products. Your feedback helps developers identify and fix bugs, improve usability, and ultimately create better products for end users.

Disadvantages of Website and App Testing:

◇ **Low Earnings per Test:** The pay outs for individual testing sessions can be modest, often ranging from a few dollars to tens of dollars depending on the platform and test complexity. Generating a substantial income solely through testing requires participation in a high volume of tests.

◇ **Inconsistent Work Availability:** Testing opportunities may not be readily available all the time. The frequency of projects can vary depending on the platform you use and your profile information.

◇ **Can Be Repetitive:** Testing similar types of websites or apps can become repetitive over time, especially if you participate in frequent testing sessions.

◇ **Technical Requirements:** While extensive technical knowledge isn't typically required, you'll need a reliable internet connection, a working computer or mobile device depending on the test type, and the ability to record your screen and voice for some testing sessions.

Who Might Benefit from Website and App Testing?

◈ **Individuals Seeking Flexible Income:** If you're looking for a way to earn some extra cash with a flexible schedule, website and app testing can be a convenient option.

◈ **Tech-Savvy Individuals with Observant Eyes:** Those comfortable navigating digital interfaces and have a keen eye for detail are well-suited for identifying usability issues and providing constructive feedback.

◈ **Early Career Professionals or Students:** Gain valuable experience in the tech industry by participating in website and app testing. This can be a good entry point to learn about user experience (UX) design principles and how user feedback shapes the development process.

Alternatives to Consider:

◈ **Microtasking Platforms:** Similar to testing, microtasking platforms offer small rewards for completing simple online tasks. Earnings might be slightly higher than some testing gigs, but the tasks can be repetitive.

◈ **Freelancing Platforms:** If you possess specific skills like user experience (UX) design or web development, consider offering your services on freelance platforms. This requires more upfront effort and skills, but the earning potential is significantly higher compared to testing.

◈ **Online Tutoring:** Share your knowledge and expertise by tutoring students online. Platforms connect tutors with students in various subjects. Earnings depend on your qualifications and experience, but offer a higher earning potential than testing with a direct impact on others.

The Bottom Line:

Website and app testing offers a flexible way to contribute to the digital world and earn some extra income. However, the earning potential is generally low. Carefully consider the time commitment involved versus the potential rewards before diving in. Explore alternative options that might provide a better return on your time and effort in the long run, especially if your goal is to generate a significant income stream.

Unveiling the World of Website and App Testing

⬦ **Testing Websites and Apps:** Companies seek user feedback to improve their websites and apps. Testing involves navigating interfaces, completing tasks, and reporting bugs or suggesting improvements. Earnings per test vary, but it's generally considered a low-earning activity. The digital landscape thrives on user experience. Companies constantly strive to improve their websites and apps, and that's where website and app testers come in. These testers act as digital guinea pigs, navigating interfaces, completing tasks, and providing valuable feedback to help developers identify and address usability issues. While contributing to the creation of polished digital products is rewarding, it's important to understand the realities of website and app testing, particularly regarding earning potential. Let's delve deeper into this field, exploring its advantages, disadvantages, and who might find it a suitable fit.

ADVANTAGES OF WEBSITE and App Testing:

Flexible Work Schedule: Testing opportunities are often available on flexible schedules. Fit testing sessions around your existing commitments, making it a good option for students, stay-at-home parents, or those seeking a side hustle.

No Prior Experience Required: Unlike some online income avenues, website and app testing generally doesn't require specific technical skills. The ability to follow instructions, provide clear feedback, and navigate user interfaces effectively are the key qualities companies seek.

Remote Work Opportunity: Testing can be done from the comfort of your own home, eliminating the need for commutes or adhering to a specific work environment.

Contribute to Product Development: Play a role in shaping the user experience of digital products. Your feedback helps developers identify and fix bugs, improve usability, and ultimately create better products for end users.

Disadvantages of Website and App Testing:

Low Earnings per Test: The pay outs for individual testing sessions can be modest, often ranging from a few dollars to tens of dollars depending on the platform and test complexity. Generating a substantial income solely through testing requires participation in a high volume of tests.

Inconsistent Work Availability: Testing opportunities may not be readily available all the time. The frequency of projects can vary depending on the platform you use and your profile information.

Can Be Repetitive: Testing similar types of websites or apps can become repetitive over time, especially if you participate in frequent testing sessions.

Technical Requirements: While extensive technical knowledge isn't typically required, you'll need a reliable internet connection, a working computer or mobile device depending on the test type, and the ability to record your screen and voice for some testing sessions.

Who Might Benefit from Website and App Testing?

INDIVIDUALS SEEKING Flexible Income: If you're looking for a way to earn some extra cash with a flexible schedule, website and app testing can be a convenient option.

Tech-Savvy Individuals with Observant Eyes: Those comfortable navigating digital interfaces and have a keen eye for detail are well-suited for identifying usability issues and providing constructive feedback.

Early Career Professionals or Students: Gain valuable experience in the tech industry by participating in website and app testing. This can be a good entry point to learn about user experience (UX) design principles and how user feedback shapes the development process.

Alternatives to Consider:

Microtasking Platforms: Similar to testing, microtasking platforms offer small rewards for completing simple online tasks. Earnings might be slightly higher than some testing gigs, but the tasks can be repetitive.

Freelancing Platforms: If you possess specific skills like user experience (UX) design or web development, consider offering your services on freelance platforms. This requires more upfront effort and skills, but the earning potential is significantly higher compared to testing.

Online Tutoring: Share your knowledge and expertise by tutoring students online. Platforms connect tutors with students in various subjects. Earnings depend on your qualifications and experience, but offer a higher earning potential than testing with a direct impact on others.

The Bottom Line:

Website and app testing offers a flexible way to contribute to the digital world and earn some extra income. However, the earning potential is generally low. Carefully consider the time commitment involved versus the potential rewards before diving in. Explore alternative options that might provide a better return on your time and effort in the long run, especially if your goal is to generate a significant income stream.

The Allure and Limitations of Earning Through Games

PLAYING GAMES: A small niche of online games allows players to earn rewards or even in-game currency that can be converted into real-world money. However, the earning potential is typically minimal and often requires significant time investment. The allure of turning playtime into real income is undeniable. A small niche of online games caters to this desire, offering players rewards or in-game currency that can be converted into real-world money. While the concept sounds like a dream come true for gamers, it's crucial to understand the limitations of this approach before dedicating significant time and effort. Let's delve deeper into the world of games with earning potential, exploring the pros and cons, and who might find this a suitable fit.

The Enticing Side of Play-to-Earn Games:

Merge Your Passions: Gamers can potentially monetize their hobby by playing games they already enjoy. This can feel less like work and more like a fun way to earn some extra cash.

Accessibility: Some play-to-earn games require minimal upfront investment, making them accessible to a broad audience.

Community Building: Certain games foster a strong sense of community, allowing players to connect, strategize, and potentially earn together.

Potential for High Earners: While uncommon, there are documented cases of players generating significant income through play-to-earn games. However, these cases often involve a combination of exceptional skill, strategic investment, and a large time commitment.

The Reality Check of Play-to-Earn Games:

Low Earning Potential for Most: The reality for most players is that earnings are typically minimal. The time invested rarely translates to a substantial income, especially after factoring in the opportunity cost of pursuing other income-generating activities.

Time Commitment: Generating any meaningful income through play-to-earn games often requires a significant time investment. Be prepared to grind through repetitive tasks or devote a considerable amount of time to mastering the game's mechanics.

Market Fluctuations and Volatility: The in-game currency or rewards earned in play-to-earn games can be subject to market fluctuations. Their real-world value can be volatile, leading to potential losses if you're not cautious.

Game Sustainability Concerns: The long-term sustainability of play-to-earn games is yet to be proven. Some games experience decline in player base or economic viability over time, potentially rendering invested time and effort worthless.

Who Might Enjoy Play-to-Earn Games

(Despite the Limitations)

HARD-CORE GAMERS WITH Time to Spare: If you're already a dedicated gamer who spends a significant amount of time playing games, and are aware of the limitations of earning potential, play-to-earn games might add a layer of gamification to your existing hobby.

Early Adopters with High Risk Tolerance: The play-to-earn space is still evolving, and there's a potential for early adopters to benefit from successful game economies. However, this involves a high degree of risk tolerance and the understanding that the market is volatile.

Alternatives to Consider:

Freelancing Platforms: Offer your gaming skills, like strategy development, level design, or esports coaching, on freelance platforms. This leverages your gaming knowledge while offering a potentially higher earning potential.

Content Creation: Stream your gameplay, create tutorials or reviews of play-to-earn games, or build a community around your gaming expertise. Monetize your content through advertising, sponsorships, or affiliate marketing.

Esports Tournaments: If you possess exceptional skills in a particular game, participate in esports tournaments with real-world prize money. However, this requires a high level of dedication and competitive spirit.

The Bottom Line:

Playing games to earn money can be an enticing prospect, but approach it with a dose of realism. The earning potential for most players is minimal, and the time commitment can be significant. Carefully weigh the pros and cons before diving in, and consider alternative options that might provide a better return on your time and effort, especially if your goal is to generate a substantial income stream. Remember, gaming can be a fun and engaging hobby, but relying on it solely for income can be risky and unsustainable.

Flexibility with Limited Earnings Potential

MICROTASKS AND CONTENT Creation: Platforms offer small payments for completing microtasks like data entry, image tagging, or writing short text pieces. While flexible and requiring minimal skills, the earnings per task are very low, making it difficult to generate a sustainable income. Microtasks and content creation platforms have emerged as a way to earn money online with seemingly minimal effort. These platforms offer bite-sized jobs like data entry, image tagging, writing short product descriptions, or completing surveys. While the flexibility and low barrier to entry are attractive, it's crucial to understand the realities of micro work before investing your time and energy. Let's delve deeper into this domain, exploring its advantages and disadvantages, and determining who might find it a suitable fit.

The Allure of Microtasks:

Flexibility and Convenience: Microtasks can be completed anytime, anywhere with an internet connection. Fit them around your existing commitments, making them ideal for stay-at-home parents, students, or those seeking a side hustle.

Low Barrier to Entry: No special skills or qualifications are typically required. Most platforms require basic computer literacy and the ability to follow instructions.

Passive Income Potential: While the earnings per task are low, completing them consistently can contribute to a small stream of passive income. Think of it like collecting digital change that accumulates over time.

Variety of Tasks: Many platforms offer a diverse range of microtasks, allowing you to choose activities that align with your interests and skills.

The Limitations of Microwork:

Low Earnings per Task: The reality is that microwork pays very little. Individual tasks might earn you mere cents, making it difficult to generate a substantial income unless you complete a very high volume of tasks.

Time Commitment vs. Reward: The time spent completing a large number of microtasks to reach a decent earning level might be better utilized in pursuing other income generation opportunities with a higher return.

Repetitive and Mind-Numbing Work: Microtasks can be monotonous and repetitive, especially if done for extended periods. The lack of challenge or creative input can lead to boredom and disengagement.

Unstable Work Availability: The availability of microtasks can fluctuate depending on the platform and your profile information. There's no guarantee of a steady stream of work.

Who Might Benefit from Microtasks?

INDIVIDUALS SEEKING Supplemental Income: If you're looking for a way to earn a few extra bucks here and there, and have time to spare, microwork can be a convenient option. However, don't expect to replace your full-time income with this approach.

Stay-at-Home Parents or Students with Flexible Schedules: The flexibility of microtasks can be valuable for those with time constraints. Complete tasks during nap times or between classes to generate a small additional income stream.

Those New to Online Work: Microtasks offer a low-risk entry point to the world of online work. You can gain experience with different types of online tasks and platforms before venturing into more complex areas.

Alternatives to Consider:

Website and App Testing: Similar to microtasks, website and app testing platforms offer small rewards for completing user testing sessions. The earnings per test might be slightly higher than some microtasks, and the work can involve providing valuable feedback and contributing to product development.

Freelancing Platforms: If you possess specific skills like writing, editing, graphic design, or programming, consider freelancing platforms. Offer your services to clients and set your own rates. This requires more upfront effort to establish your profile and secure projects, but the earning potential is significantly higher compared to microtasks.

Online Tutoring: Share your knowledge and expertise by tutoring students online. Platforms connect tutors with students in various subjects. Earnings depend on your qualifications and experience, but offer a higher earning potential than microtasks with a direct impact on others.

The Bottom Line:

Microtasks offer a taste of online income generation with minimal upfront investment. However, the low earnings make it an unsustainable income source. Carefully consider the time commitment involved versus the potential rewards before diving in. Explore alternative options that might provide a better return on your time and effort in the long run, especially if your goal is to generate a substantial income stream. Remember, microwork can be a convenient way to earn a little extra on the side, but it shouldn't be your primary income strategy.

Unleashing Your Skills and Building a Thriving Online Career

FREELANCING: Offer your skills and expertise as a freelancer on online marketplaces. Writers, editors, graphic designers, programmers, and virtual assistants can find freelance work in various fields. Earnings depend on your skills, experience, and the complexity of projects you undertake. Freelancing has emerged as a powerful force in the modern workforce, empowering individuals to leverage their skills and expertise for a more flexible and potentially lucrative career path. Bypassing the traditional employer-employee dynamic, freelancers offer their services directly to clients, setting their own rates, and managing their own workflows. While enticing, this path requires dedication, self-marketing savvy, and a strategic approach. Here's a deeper look into the world of freelancing, exploring its advantages, challenges, and factors to consider before embarking on this exciting journey.

The Allure of Freelancing:

Be Your Own Boss: Enjoy the freedom and autonomy of setting your own work schedule, choosing your clients, and managing your workload.

Work from Anywhere: Untether yourself from a physical office. Freelance with the flexibility to work from home, a co-working space, or even while traveling the world.

Diverse Project Opportunities: Freelancing opens doors to a vast array of projects across various industries. Expand your skillset, explore new niches, and keep your work dynamic and engaging.

Earning Potential Based on Skills: Your income is directly tied to your skills and experience. As you build your reputation and expertise, you can command higher rates and increase your earning potential.

Work-Life Balance: Freelancing allows you to tailor your work hours around your personal life, creating a better work-life balance compared to traditional employment.

Challenges and Considerations:

Self-Discipline and Time Management: Freelancing requires strong self-discipline to stay focused, meet deadlines, and manage multiple projects simultaneously.

Client Acquisition and Marketing: The onus falls on you to find clients and market your services effectively. Developing strong communication and sales skills is crucial for building a successful freelance career.

Financial Fluctuation: Freelance income can be inconsistent, especially when starting out. Be prepared for periods of low income and develop strategies for financial planning and budgeting.

Benefits and Security: Freelancers are typically responsible for their own health insurance, social security contributions, and other benefits typically offered by traditional employers.

Isolation and Self-Motivation: Working independently can lead to feelings of isolation. Building a network of fellow freelancers or joining online communities can help combat this.

Who Thrives in Freelancing?

SELF-MOTIVATED AND Results-Oriented Individuals: Freelancing demands a high degree of self-motivation and the ability to deliver high-quality work independently.

Skilled Communicators and Marketers: Being able to articulate your value proposition, negotiate rates, and build strong client relationships is essential for success.

Time Management Masters: Freelancing necessitates effective time management skills to juggle multiple projects, meet deadlines, and maintain a healthy work-life balance.

Adaptable and Lifelong Learners: The freelance landscape is constantly evolving. The ability to adapt to new technologies, market trends, and client needs is crucial for long-term success.

Taking the First Step towards a Fulfilling Freelancing Career:

Identify Your Skills and Niche: Carefully assess your strengths and areas of expertise. Identify a niche market where your skills are in high demand.

Build a Strong Online Presence: Create a professional portfolio website or online profiles showcasing your past work and client testimonials.

Develop Your Marketing Strategy: Network with potential clients, leverage online platforms to find freelance work, and utilize social media marketing to promote your services.

Set Competitive Rates: Research industry standards and set pricing that reflects your value proposition while remaining competitive in the market.

Deliver Exceptional Service: Prioritize client satisfaction and exceed expectations. This builds trust, fosters long-term client relationships, and generates positive word-of-mouth referrals.

Freelancing offers a compelling path to a fulfilling and financially rewarding career. By understanding its advantages and challenges, carefully planning your approach, and continuously honing your skills, you can thrive in this dynamic and exciting work environment.

How Affiliate Marketing Works

AFFILIATE MARKETING: Promote other companies' products or services on your website or social media channels. Earn a commission for every sale generated through your unique affiliate link. Success relies on building a targeted audience and effectively promoting relevant products.

Join an Affiliate Program: Companies offering affiliate programs provide unique tracking links or codes for their products. Whenever someone clicks on your link and completes a purchase, the sale is attributed to you, and you earn a commission.

Promote Products You Believe In: Affiliate marketing thrives on authenticity. Choose products or services that resonate with your target audience and that you genuinely recommend.

Content is King (or Queen): Create valuable content on your website, blog, or social media channels that showcases the benefits of the products you promote. This could take the form of blog posts, reviews, tutorials, or social media recommendations.

Targeted Audience is Key: Identify your niche audience and tailor your content and marketing efforts to their specific needs and interests. The more targeted your approach, the higher the conversion rate (visitors who turn into paying customers) for your affiliate links.

Multiple Streams of Promotion: Explore various channels to reach your target audience. Utilize a combination of website content, social media marketing, email marketing, and even paid advertising strategies to maximize reach and brand awareness.

Factors Influencing Affiliate Marketing Success:

Building a Loyal Audience: Success hinges on cultivating a trusting and engaged audience who values your recommendations. Focus on providing high-quality content, fostering genuine interactions, and establishing yourself as a reliable source of information within your niche.

Strategic Content Creation: Content should not be solely promotional. Educate, entertain, and inform your audience while subtly weaving in the value proposition of the products you promote.

Transparency and Disclosure: Always disclose that you're using affiliate links and explain how it benefits both you and your audience. Transparency builds trust and strengthens your relationships with your followers.

Data tracking and Optimization: Utilize analytics tools to track user behavior and measure the performance of your affiliate campaigns. This data allows you to refine your approach, identify what resonates with your audience, and optimize your content for better conversions.

Patience and Persistence: Building a successful affiliate marketing business takes time and consistent effort. Don't get discouraged if results aren't immediate. Stay focused, keep creating valuable content, and continually refine your strategies for long-term success.

Who Can Benefit from Affiliate Marketing?

CONTENT CREATORS (BLOGGERS, YouTubers, etc.): If you already have an established audience interested in a particular niche, affiliate marketing allows you to monetize your content by recommending relevant products or services.

Social Media Influencers: Leverage your social media following to promote affiliate products that align with your audience's interests. Build trust and authenticity to encourage clicks and conversions.

Website Owners: Drive traffic to your website through valuable content and strategically place affiliate links within your content to generate income.

The Bottom Line:

Affiliate marketing offers a viable path to online income generation. However, it requires building trust with your audience, creating high-quality content, and strategically promoting relevant products. By understanding the core principles, success factors, and the dedication required, you can turn affiliate marketing into a rewarding endeavour that complements your existing online presence. Remember, focus on providing value to your audience, prioritize transparency, and continuously adapt your strategies to maximize your earning potential.

Unveiling the Realities of Being a Social Media Influencer

SOCIAL MEDIA INFLUENCER: Build a large following on social media platforms and leverage your influence to promote brands or products. Earnings come through sponsored posts, brand collaborations, or affiliate marketing. Growing a significant audience takes time and consistent effort. The world of social media influencers seems glamorous – jet-setting lifestyles, designer collaborations, and seemingly effortless income. But behind the carefully curated feeds lies a reality of dedicated work, strategic planning, and a commitment to building a loyal audience. If you dream of leveraging your social media presence to become an influencer, here's a deeper look at this career path, exploring the different avenues for income generation, the challenges you might face, and who is best suited for this dynamic field.

Monetization Strategies for Social Media Influencers:

Sponsored Posts and Brand Collaborations: Partner with brands to create sponsored content promoting their products or services. This could involve product placements, reviews, social media mentions, or even attending branded events.

Affiliate Marketing: Similar to other online income streams, promote products through affiliate links and earn commissions for every sale generated through your unique link.

Selling Your Own Products or Services: Leverage your established audience to launch your own product line, merchandise, or even offer consulting services within your niche.

Live streaming and Exclusive Content: Platforms like Instagram Live and Patreon allow influencers to connect directly with fans and offer exclusive content in exchange for subscriptions or donations.

Challenges of Being a Social Media Influencer:

Building a Loyal Audience Takes Time: Growing a significant following requires consistent content creation, audience engagement, and a strategic approach to reach new followers. Be prepared to invest time and effort before seeing significant results.

Maintaining Content Consistency: Staying relevant and engaging requires regularly creating high-quality content that resonates with your audience. This can be a demanding task, especially as your audience grows and expectations evolve.

Adapting to Algorithm Changes: Social media platforms constantly update their algorithms, impacting how content is displayed. Successful influencers need to stay informed and adapt their strategies to maintain visibility and reach.

Coping with Negative Comments and Online Scrutiny: The online world can be harsh. Influencers often face criticism and negativity. Developing a thick skin and maintaining a positive online presence are crucial.

Maintaining Authenticity While Working with Brands: Finding a balance between promoting brands and staying true to your values is essential. Audiences can easily detect inauthenticity, so ensure brand partnerships align with your genuine interests and recommendations.

Who Thrives as a Social Media Influencer?

CREATIVE AND ENGAGING Storytellers: The ability to capture attention, tell compelling stories, and create visually appealing content is paramount for attracting and retaining followers.

Community Builders: Social media thrives on interaction. Successful influencers foster a sense of community, engage with their audience, and respond to comments and messages to build genuine connections.

Trendsetters with a Niche Expertise: Having a distinct voice and a well-defined niche allows you to attract a targeted audience interested in your specific content and recommendations.

Thick-Skinned and Adaptable: The ability to handle criticism and adapt to platform changes is essential for navigating the ever-evolving social media landscape.

Passionate and Persistent: Building a successful social media presence takes time and dedication. Genuine passion for your niche and the persistence to keep creating content are key drivers of long-term success.

The Bottom Line:

Becoming a social media influencer can be a rewarding path, but it's not a get-rich-quick scheme. Success requires strategic planning, consistent effort, and a commitment to building trust with your audience. If you possess the creativity, dedication, and passion to navigate the ever-changing social media landscape, influencer marketing can be a fulfilling way to turn your online presence into a viable career. Remember, authenticity is key. Focus on providing valuable content to your audience, prioritize genuine connections, and continuously adapt your strategies to thrive in the dynamic world of social media influence.

Unveiling the World of Online Tutoring

ONLINE TUTORING: Share your knowledge and expertise by tutoring students online in various subjects. Platforms connect tutors with students, and earnings depend on your qualifications, experience, and the subjects you tutor. The internet has revolutionized education, and online tutoring platforms have emerged as a powerful tool for both students seeking academic support and tutors eager to share their knowledge and expertise. Imagine connecting with students from across the globe, tailoring your teaching approach to individual needs, and making a positive impact on their learning journeys – that's the essence of online tutoring. Before diving in, let's explore the advantages and considerations of this rewarding career path, along with who might find it a perfect fit.

The Allure of Online Tutoring:

Flexibility and Work-Life Balance: Set your own schedule and work from the comfort of your home. This flexibility is ideal for students, stay-at-home parents, or anyone seeking a side hustle that fits around their existing commitments.

Global Reach: Connect with students from all over the world, fostering intercultural understanding and expanding your impact as an educator.

Impactful and Rewarding: Witnessing students grasp concepts and overcome challenges can be incredibly rewarding. Online tutoring allows you to make a tangible difference in their academic success.

Diverse Subject Areas: Platforms offer tutoring opportunities in a wide range of subjects, allowing you to leverage your expertise in areas you're passionate about.

No Classroom Management Hassles: Focus on delivering high-quality instruction without the distractions of classroom management.

Considerations for Online Tutors:

Subject Expertise and Strong Communication Skills: A thorough understanding of the subjects you tutor and the ability to explain complex concepts clearly are essential.

Engaging Teaching Style: Captivate students through online platforms. Utilize interactive tools, whiteboards, and effective communication to keep them engaged and motivated.

Technology Requirements: Reliable internet connection, a webcam, and a headset are necessary for conducting online tutoring sessions effectively.

Platform Specificity: Different platforms have varying requirements, fee structures, and student demographics. Research and choose a platform that aligns with your qualifications, teaching style, and target audience.

Time Commitment: While flexible, online tutoring requires dedication to prepare lessons, meet with students regularly, and provide quality feedback.

Who Thrives in Online Tutoring?

ENTHUSIASTIC EDUCATORS and Subject Matter Experts: If you possess a passion for a particular subject and enjoy guiding others towards understanding, online tutoring allows you to share your knowledge and make a positive impact.

Excellent Communicators and Patient Mentors: The ability to explain complex concepts clearly, break down learning barriers, and offer constructive feedback are crucial for success.

Tech-Savvy Individuals: Comfort with online learning platforms, video conferencing tools, and digital content creation tools is essential for a smooth tutoring experience.

Time Management Masters: Juggling student schedules, lesson planning, and administrative tasks requires strong time management skills to maintain a productive workflow.

Self-Motivated and Results-Oriented: Setting your own schedule and managing your workload demands a high degree of self-motivation and a commitment to student success.

The Bottom Line:

Online tutoring offers a flexible and rewarding way to share your knowledge and make a difference in the lives of students worldwide. By leveraging your expertise, developing engaging teaching methods, and embracing technology, you can build a successful online tutoring career. Remember, fostering a love of learning and guiding students towards academic achievement is the cornerstone of online tutoring. If you possess the passion, dedication, and the right skillset, this path can be a fulfilling way to turn your knowledge into a positive impact on the next generation of learners.

Unveiling the Content Creator's Journey - Blogging and Vlogging for Passion and Profit

◇ **Blogging and Vlogging:** Create informative or entertaining content on a blog or YouTube channel. Monetize your content through advertising, sponsorships, affiliate marketing, or selling your own products or services. Building a successful blog or vlog requires time, dedication, and a strong content strategy. The world of blogging and vlogging has exploded, empowering individuals to share their voices, document their passions, and even build thriving online businesses. From insightful blog posts to captivating video content, creators leverage these platforms to entertain, educate, and connect with a global audience. But behind the seemingly effortless vlogs and polished blog posts lies a dedication to content creation, audience engagement, and strategic planning. Let's delve deeper into the world of blogging and vlogging, exploring the different avenues for monetization, the challenges you might face, and who is best suited for this exciting path.

THE ENTICING FACETS of Blogging and Vlogging:

◇ **Be Your Own Boss:** Craft your own content calendar, set your own schedule, and express your unique voice and creativity.

◇ **Turn Your Passion into a Platform:** Share your knowledge, hobbies, or interests with the world. Build a community around your passions and connect with like-minded individuals.

⬧ **Monetization Potential:** While not an overnight endeavor, successful blogs and vlogs can be monetized through advertising, affiliate marketing, sponsored content, or even selling your own products or services.

⬧ **Location Independence:** Work from anywhere with an internet connection. Unleash your creativity and share your content with a global audience, transcending geographical boundaries.

⬧ **Building a Personal Brand:** Establish yourself as an expert in your niche and leverage your blog or vlog as a platform to showcase your expertise and build a loyal following.

The Realities of Building a Successful Blog or Vlog:

⬧ **Content is King (or Queen):** Creating high-quality, engaging content consistently is paramount. Research your target audience, identify their needs, and deliver valuable information or entertainment that keeps them coming back for more.

⬧ **SEO Optimization:** For blogs, understanding Search Engine Optimization (SEO) helps your content rank higher in search results, driving organic traffic to your website.

⬧ **Marketing and Promotion:** Building an audience takes effort. Utilize social media marketing, email marketing, and collaborations with other creators to promote your content and reach new viewers or readers.

⬦ **Staying Ahead of the Curve:** The online landscape is constantly evolving. Be prepared to adapt your content strategy, embrace new trends, and keep your finger on the pulse of your niche to stay relevant.

⬦ **Time Commitment and Patience:** Building a successful blog or vlog takes time and dedication. Don't get discouraged by slow initial growth. Stay focused, keep creating valuable content, and celebrate your milestones along the way.

Who Can Thrive in the Blogging and Vlogging World?

◈ **Passionate Storytellers:** The ability to captivate your audience through compelling narratives, whether written or visual, is key to keeping them engaged.

◈ **Content Creators with a Strategic Mind-set:** Balancing informative content with a monetization strategy is crucial for long-term success.

◈ **Tech-Savvy Individuals:** Understanding basic content creation tools, video editing software (for vlogs), and website management skills are essential.

◈ **Community Builders:** Foster interaction with your audience. Respond to comments, host discussions, and actively participate in conversations to build a loyal following.

◈ **Lifelong Learners:** Be prepared to continuously learn new skills, adapt to changing algorithms, and stay updated on trends within your niche to maintain a competitive edge.

THE BOTTOM LINE:

Blogging and vlogging offer a unique blend of creative expression and potential income generation. However, it requires dedication, strategic planning, and a commitment to delivering high-quality content. If you possess the passion, creativity, and willingness to learn, this path can be a fulfilling way to share your voice with the world and potentially turn your blog or vlog into a thriving online venture. Remember, focus on creating valuable content, consistently engage with your audience, and embrace the journey of growth and learning as you build your online presence.

Building Your Thriving Online Store

◈ **Ecommerce:** Sell physical or digital products through your own online store. Manage inventory, marketing, and customer service. Success hinges on identifying a profitable niche, effective marketing strategies, and providing a seamless customer experience. E-commerce has revolutionized retail, empowering individuals to become entrepreneurs and establish their own online stores. This exciting realm allows you to sell physical products directly to consumers, or offer downloadable digital goods – all from the comfort of your home or office. However, venturing into e-commerce requires careful planning, strategic execution, and a commitment to providing exceptional customer service. Let's delve into the nitty-gritty of e-commerce, exploring the key factors for success, the different business models, and who might find this path fulfilling.

ESSENTIALS FOR BUILDING a Successful E-commerce Store:

◈ **Identifying a Profitable Niche:** Conduct thorough market research to identify a gap in the market or a niche with a passionate customer base. Focus on a specific product category or cater to a particular audience with unique needs.

◈ **Choosing the Right E-commerce Platform:** Numerous platforms cater to e-commerce businesses. Research and choose a platform that aligns with your technical expertise, budget, scalability needs, and features like product management tools, marketing integrations, and payment processing options.

◇ **Crafting a Compelling Brand Identity:** Develop a unique brand that resonates with your target audience. This includes your logo, website design, brand voice, and overall customer experience.

◇ **Creating High-Quality Product Listings:** Compelling product descriptions, professional product photos from multiple angles, and detailed specifications are crucial for converting website visitors into paying customers.

◇ **Effective Marketing Strategies:** Utilize a combination of organic search engine optimization (SEO), social media marketing, pay-per-click advertising (PPC), email marketing, and influencer marketing to drive traffic to your online store.

◇ **Seamless Customer Experience:** Prioritize a user-friendly website, secure payment gateways, efficient order fulfilment processes, and exceptional customer service to build trust and encourage repeat business.

◇ **Data-Driven Decision Making:** Track website traffic, analyze customer behavior, and monitor key metrics like conversion rates and customer acquisition costs. Use this data to refine your marketing strategies, optimize product offerings, and continuously improve your online store.

E-commerce Business Models:

◇ **Dropshipping:** Partner with a dropshipping supplier who stores, packs, and ships products directly to your customers. This eliminates the need for you to manage inventory or handle fulfilment.

◇ **Wholesaling:** Purchase products in bulk at wholesale prices and then resell them on your online store at a mark-up. Requires upfront investment in inventory but offers higher profit margins.

◇ **Private Label Products:** Design and manufacture your own unique products or partner with a manufacturer to create custom-labelled products. Offers greater control over branding and potentially higher profit margins but requires upfront investment and product development expertise.

Who Thrives in E-commerce?

◈ **Highly Motivated and Results-Oriented Individuals:** Building a successful e-commerce business requires dedication, a willingness to learn, and the ability to adapt to changing market trends.

◈ **Tech-Savvy Entrepreneurs:** Understanding e-commerce platforms, basic website maintenance, and marketing tools is necessary for managing your online store effectively.

◈ **Creative and Resourceful Problem Solvers:** From managing inventory to resolving customer issues, e-commerce entrepreneurs need to be resourceful and capable of tackling unforeseen challenges.

◈ **Data Analysts and Marketing Mavens:** The ability to analyze data, identify trends, and implement effective marketing strategies is crucial for attracting customers and driving sales.

◈ **Customer Service Champions:** Providing exceptional customer service is vital for building trust and fostering customer loyalty.

THE BOTTOM LINE:

E-commerce offers a dynamic and potentially lucrative path to entrepreneurship. However, it requires careful planning, strategic execution, and a commitment to continuously learning and adapting. By identifying a profitable niche, establishing a strong brand identity, and prioritizing the customer experience, you can build a thriving online store that competes in the ever-evolving world of e-commerce. Remember, success hinges on a blend of entrepreneurial spirit, data-driven decision making, and a relentless focus on providing exceptional customer service. So, if you possess the drive, creativity, and willingness to learn, e-commerce might be the perfect platform to turn your entrepreneurial vision into a thriving online reality.

Unveiling the World of Investing

Growing Your Wealth through Calculated Risks

◇ **Investing:** Invest in stocks, bonds, real estate, or other financial instruments. While potentially lucrative, investing carries inherent risks and requires financial knowledge and risk tolerance. Always conduct thorough research before making any investment decisions. Investing presents a powerful tool for building wealth over time. By strategically allocating your money across various financial instruments, you can harness the potential of the market to achieve your long-term financial goals. This realm, however, is not without its complexities. Understanding the different asset classes, managing risk effectively, and possessing a healthy dose of patience are all crucial for navigating the investment landscape. Let's embark on a deeper exploration of investing, delving into the different asset classes, investment strategies, and who might find this path to financial growth appealing.

THE INVESTMENT LANDSCAPE: A Plethora of Choices

◇ **Stocks (Equities):** Ownership shares in publicly traded companies. Offer the potential for capital appreciation (stock price increase) and dividend income (company payouts). However, stock prices can be volatile, and you could lose money.

◇ **Bonds:** Loans you make to governments or corporations. Generally considered less risky than stocks, bonds provide a fixed interest rate (coupon) paid at regular intervals until the bond matures.

◈ **Mutual Funds and Exchange-Traded Funds (ETFs):** These pooled investment vehicles allow you to invest in a basket of stocks, bonds, or other assets. Offer diversification (spreading risk across multiple investments) and professional management by fund managers.

◈ **Real Estate:** Investing in physical property, either directly by purchasing properties or indirectly through Real Estate Investment Trusts (REITs). Can generate rental income and potential for property value appreciation, but requires significant capital and carries management responsibilities.

◈ **Alternative Investments:** These encompass a wider range of assets such as commodities (gold, oil), private equity (investing in non-public companies), and hedge funds (actively managed investment vehicles with higher risk profiles). Generally require a higher level of investment expertise and are not suitable for all investors.

Crafting Your Investment Strategy:

◈ **Define Your Investment Goals:** Are you saving for retirement, a down payment on a house, or a child's education? Understanding your goals helps determine your investment timeline (short-term vs. long-term) and risk tolerance.

◈ **Risk Tolerance Assessment:** How comfortable are you with potential losses? Younger investors with a longer time horizon can typically tolerate more risk in pursuit of higher potential returns. As you approach retirement, you may prioritize capital preservation and shift towards less volatile investments.

⬦ **Asset Allocation:** Diversification is key. Spread your investments across different asset classes to mitigate risk. The ideal asset allocation depends on your risk tolerance, investment goals, and time horizon. There are various asset allocation models you can research, or consult a financial advisor for personalized guidance.

⬦ **Rebalancing Your Portfolio:** Over time, the value of different asset classes will fluctuate. Periodically rebalance your portfolio to maintain your desired asset allocation and manage risk exposure.

Who Should Consider Investing?

◈ **Individuals with Long-Term Financial Goals:** Investing shines over extended periods. If you have goals that are several years or decades away, investing allows your money to grow through the power of compound interest (earning interest on your interest).

◈ **Those Willing to Learn and Research:** The financial markets can be complex. While formal education isn't essential, dedicating time to learn about different investment options, conducting thorough research, and staying informed about economic trends is crucial for making sound investment decisions.

Cultivating Your Investment Expertise: Resources for the Aspiring Investor

THE VAST WORLD OF INVESTING can seem intimidating at first glance. Complex financial jargon, fluctuating markets, and an overwhelming array of investment options can leave you feeling unsure where to begin. However, the good news is that formal education isn't a prerequisite for becoming a savvy investor. With dedication, a willingness to learn, and a commitment to ongoing research, you can equip yourself with the knowledge and tools necessary to make informed investment decisions. Here's a roadmap to empower yourself as an investor, along with suggestions on where you can embark on your financial learning journey:

Building Your Investment Knowledge Base:

◈ **Online Resources:** Numerous reputable websites and financial blogs offer valuable investment information. Look for sites with a strong track record, unbiased content, and a focus on investor education. Here are a few starting points:

o Investopedia (https://www.investopedia.com/): A comprehensive online encyclopedia covering all aspects of finance and investing, with articles, tutorials, and investor guides.

o The Motley Fool (https://www.fool.com/): Provides financial news, analysis, and educational content, with a focus on long-term investing strategies.

o Khan Academy (khanacademy.org): Offers a free course on personal finance, including a unit on investing basics.

◈ **Books:** A wealth of investment books cater to different experience levels. Start with beginner-friendly guides that explain core concepts and investment strategies. Here are a few suggestions:

o "The Intelligent Investor" by Benjamin Graham: A classic text considered the bible of value investing.

o "A Random Walk Down Wall Street" by Burton Malkiel: Debunks the notion of market timing and advocates for a long-term, diversified investment approach.

o "I Will Teach You to Be Rich" by Ramit Sethi: A practical guide to personal finance management, including a section on investing basics.

◈ **Investment Podcasts and Youtube Channels:** Stay informed and learn on the go with investment-focused podcasts and Youtube channels. These provide insights from financial experts in an engaging format. Here are a few options to explore:

o   The   Investor's   Podcast (https://www.theinvestorspodcast.com/):   In-depth interviews with successful investors and financial professionals.

o Planet Money (https://www.npr.org/sections/money/): NPR podcast that tackles complex economic concepts in a fun and accessible way, with occasional episodes on investing.

o The Finance Guy (https://m.youtube.com/c/ FinanceGuy): Youtube channel offering investment education and analysis, geared towards millennial investors.

Beyond Knowledge

Developing Your Research Skills

◇ **Annual Reports and Company Filings:** Publicly traded companies are required to file annual reports and other financial documents with the Securities and Exchange Commission (SEC) in the US. These reports offer valuable insights into a company's financial health, performance, and future plans. You can access them for free on the SEC's website (https://www.sec.gov/edgar).

◇ **Financial News and Analysis:** Stay updated on market trends, economic news, and company-specific developments by following reputable financial news sources. Look for publications and websites known for their objective reporting and in-depth analysis.

REMEMBER:

◇ **Start Small and Gradually Scale Up:** As you gain knowledge and confidence, gradually increase the complexity of your investment portfolio.

Automated Investing for the Busy or Hands-Off Investor

◈ **Consider a Robo-Advisor:** For those seeking a more hands-off approach, consider using a robo-advisor. These automated investment platforms create and manage a diversified portfolio based on your risk tolerance and investment goals. The world of investing can be exciting, but it can also feel overwhelming. Researching companies, analysing markets, and actively managing a portfolio require time, dedication, and a certain level of comfort with financial matters. What if there was a way to benefit from the potential of the market without the constant monitoring and decision-making? Enter robo-advisors – automated investment platforms designed to simplify investing for busy individuals or those seeking a hands-off approach.

HOW ROBO-ADVISORS WORK:

1. **Risk Tolerance Assessment:** Through a series of questions, robo-advisors assess your risk tolerance. This helps them determine the appropriate asset allocation for your portfolio, balancing riskier assets like stocks with more stable options like bonds.

2. **Investment Goal Setting:** Whether it's saving for retirement, a down payment on a house, or a child's education, robo-advisors consider your investment goals to tailor the investment strategy and timeline.

3. Automated Portfolio Creation and Management: Based on your risk tolerance and goals, the robo-advisor builds a diversified portfolio of ETFs (Exchange-Traded Funds) or stocks. They also handle automatic rebalancing to maintain the desired asset allocation over time.

4. Low Investment Minimums: Unlike traditional investment firms, many robo-advisors have low minimum investment requirements, making them accessible to those just starting their investment journey.

5. Low Fees: Robo-advisors typically charge a fraction of the fees compared to traditional financial advisors, making them a cost-effective option for many investors.

Who Can Benefit from a Robo-Advisor?

◈ **Busy Professionals:** If you have a demanding career and limited time, a robo-advisor can handle the investment management aspects, freeing you to focus on other priorities.

◈ **New Investors:** Robo-advisors offer a user-friendly platform and automated investment strategies, making them ideal for those taking their first steps in the investment world.

◈ **Hands-Off Investors:** If you prefer a set-it-and-forget-it approach, robo-advisors can manage your portfolio with minimal intervention from you.

Popular Robo-Advisor Options

(consider researching these or using a comparison tool to find the best fit for you):

⬦ **Betterment:** A pioneer in the robo-advisor space, Betterment offers a user-friendly platform, low fees, and a variety of account options, including tax-optimized portfolios.

⬦ **Wealthfront:** Known for its tax-efficient investing strategies and robo-advisor technology, Wealthfront caters to a range of investor needs with different account tiers.

⬦ **Schwab Intelligent Portfolios:** Leveraging the investment expertise of Charles Schwab, Schwab Intelligent Portfolios offers a robo-advisor service with low fees and access to research and educational resources.

⬦ **Vanguard Personal Advisor Services:** This robo-advisor service from Vanguard, a renowned investment provider, caters to investors with a higher minimum investment but offers personalized advice and human interaction alongside automated portfolio management.

IMPORTANT CONSIDERATIONS before Choosing a Robo-Advisor:

⬦ **Investment Fees:** Compare the annual management fees charged by different robo-advisors. While generally lower than traditional advisors, fees can still impact your returns.

◈ **Account Minimums:** Some robo-advisors require a minimum investment amount to open an account. Choose one that aligns with your current investment capital.

◈ **Investment Options:** Understand the types of assets (stocks, bonds, ETFs) the robo-advisor uses to build your portfolio.

◈ **Customer Service:** Consider the level of customer support offered by the robo-advisor, especially if you value occasional human interaction for complex situations.

The Bottom Line:

Robo-advisors offer a convenient and cost-effective way to invest, making them a compelling option for busy individuals or those seeking a hands-off approach. By understanding how they work, who can benefit from them, and the various options available, you can make an informed decision about whether a robo-advisor is the right fit for your investment journey. Remember, it's crucial to research different robo-advisors, compare their features and fees, and ensure their investment philosophy aligns with your goals and risk tolerance before investing.

Seek Professional Guidance:

CONSULTING WITH A QUALIFIED financial advisor can be invaluable, especially for complex financial situations or personalized investment strategies. Look for a fee-based advisor who aligns with your investment goals and risk tolerance.

⬦ **Disciplined and Patient Individuals:** The market experiences ups and downs. Investors who can stay disciplined, avoid emotional decision-making, and maintain a long-term perspective are better positioned to weather market fluctuations and achieve their financial objectives.

The Bottom Line:

Investing empowers you to take control of your financial future. By dedicating time to learning, conducting thorough research, and staying informed, you can navigate the investment landscape with confidence. Remember, investing is a lifelong journey of continuous learning and adaptation. Embrace the process, stay disciplined, and enjoy the rewards of growing your wealth over time. Investing offers a compelling path towards financial security and achieving your long-term financial goals. However, it requires careful planning, a solid understanding of risk tolerance, and a commitment to ongoing education. By diversifying your portfolio, employing a well-defined strategy, and maintaining a long-term perspective, you can navigate the investment landscape and harness its potential to grow your wealth over time. Remember, responsible investing is a marathon, not a sprint. Approach it with a blend of knowledge, discipline, and patience, and you'll be well on your way to achieving financial success. Always consult with a qualified financial advisor for personalized guidance before making any investment decisions.

Thriving Online with Diverse Opportunities

THE ONLINE WORLD OFFERS a plethora of possibilities to not only survive but thrive. Here's an expanded look at some of the exciting ways you can leverage the internet to create a fulfilling and potentially lucrative online career:

1. Become a Writer:

◈ **Content is King:** Businesses are constantly seeking high-quality content to engage their audience and establish brand authority. Offer your writing skills as a freelance writer, crafting articles, blog posts, website copy, product descriptions, or even social media content. Platforms like Upwork, Fiverr, and ProBlogger can connect you with potential clients.

◈ **Niche Down for Success:** Specializing in a particular niche like healthcare, technology, or finance allows you to develop expertise and attract clients seeking content tailored to their industry.

◈ **Explore Content Formats:** Expand your offerings beyond articles. Consider writing ebooks, white papers, case studies, or even scripts for explainer videos.

2. Do Side Gigs:

◈ **Virtual Assistant Powerhouse:** As a virtual assistant (VA), you can provide remote administrative, technical, or creative support to busy entrepreneurs and businesses. Tasks can range from scheduling appointments and managing email to social media management and data entry. Sites like Zirtual and Fancy Hands can help you find VA opportunities.

◈ **Data Entry Wizard:** Companies often require assistance with data entry tasks like product information input, customer record management, or survey data processing. If you have a keen eye for detail and strong typing skills, data entry can be a viable online income option.

◈ **Graphic Design Guru:** Do you have a knack for design? Offer freelance graphic design services online. Create logos, social media graphics, presentations, or marketing materials for clients. Platforms like Dribbble and Behance are great places to showcase your design portfolio.

3. Do Translation Work.

◈ **Bridge the Language Gap:** The world is becoming increasingly interconnected. If you're bilingual or multilingual, offer translation services online. Businesses and individuals require document translation, website localization, or even interpretation for meetings and conferences. Upwork and Freelancer.com are popular platforms for freelance translators.

◈ **Translation Specialization:** Consider specializing in a particular field like legal, medical, or technical translation to cater to a specific clientele and command higher rates.

4. Sell Your Stuff:

◈ **Embrace the Sharing Economy:** Declutter your home and give pre-loved items a new life. Platforms like Poshmark,

Depop, and ThredUp allow you to sell clothes, accessories, and other household goods to a wide audience.

⬦ **Expand Your Reach:** Don't limit yourself to just one platform. List your items on multiple online marketplaces to maximize your exposure and reach potential buyers.

⬦ **Quality Photos and Descriptions:** High-quality photos and detailed descriptions are crucial for attracting buyers. Showcase your items in their best light and provide accurate information about condition, size, and features.

5. Become a Virtual Assistant (Expanded Role):

⬦ **VA Powerhouse:** Virtual assistants can provide a wider range of services than just administrative tasks. If you have specific skills like web development, social media marketing, or bookkeeping, leverage them to offer more specialized VA services.

⬦ **Package Your Services:** Create different service packages catering to different client needs. This allows you to attract a wider clientele and potentially command higher rates.

6. Become a Twitch Streamer (and More):

⬦ **Broadcast Yourself:** Twitch is a popular platform for live streaming video game content. However, the possibilities extend beyond gaming. You can stream creative content like painting, music production, or even cooking demonstrations. Build a community, engage with your audience, and potentially earn through donations and subscriptions.

◈ **Monetize Your Streams:** Explore various monetization options on Twitch, such as subscriptions, donations (bits), and selling merchandise. Partnering with brands for sponsored streams can also be a lucrative avenue.

7. Expand Your Stock Photo Sales:

◈ **Beyond Photography:** While stock photo websites offer a platform for photographers, there's a demand for various digital assets. If you're a graphic designer or illustrator, consider creating and selling vector graphics, icons, or illustrations on these platforms.

◈ **Keyword Research:** Understanding what people are searching for is key. Use keyword research tools to identify popular search terms and create content that aligns with those keywords to increase your discoverability.

Remember: *These are just a few examples to spark your creativity. The online world is constantly evolving, presenting new opportunities to make money and build a fulfilling career. The key is to identify your skills, interests, and target audience, and leverage the power of the internet to turn your passions into profits. Be prepared to adapt,*

Choosing the Right Path:

The best online income generation method depends on your skills, interests, time commitment, and financial goals. Consider the following factors when making your choice:

- **Skills and Expertise:** Leverage your existing skills and knowledge to find suitable online work opportunities.
- **Time Commitment:** Evaluate how much time you can realistically dedicate to online income generation activities.
- **Investment Requirements:** Some options require upfront investment in equipment, software, or marketing efforts.
- **Scalability:** Consider the potential to scale your earnings over time with the chosen method.

Remember, *online success often hinges on a combination of factors: offering valuable products or services, effective marketing, and consistently delivering a positive customer experience. Explore different options, experiment to find what works best for you, and continuously adapt your strategy to maximize your online earning potential.*

About the Author

From UK Roots to Spanish Shores

I'm originally from the UK, where I spent my formative years and received my education. Life then took me on an exciting adventure to sunny Spain, where I now happily reside.

Beyond enjoying the Spanish climate and culture, I'm an avid bridge player. The strategic thinking and social aspects of the game keep me mentally sharp and provide opportunities to connect with like-minded individuals.

However, my true passion lies in the digital realm. I've had the pleasure of creating and launching several websites, immersing myself in the world of web development. But my greatest satisfaction comes from successfully developing online businesses that generate income. It's a constant learning process, but the thrill of building something from scratch and seeing it flourish is incredibly rewarding.

When I'm not glued to the screen, you might find me out on the water as a keen yachtsman. There's something truly invigorating about sailing, the feeling of freedom, and the challenge of harnessing the power of the wind.

Whether it's bridge games, building online ventures, or navigating the open seas, I'm always up for a challenge and enjoy the journey of continuous learning. Feel free to browse my work or connect with me if you share similar interests!